The Benchbook

THE BENCHBOOK

*Anecdotes from the
Lighter Side of the Law*

by Judge Jerry L. Hayes

illustrations by Chuck Ayers

THE KENT STATE UNIVERSITY PRESS

Kent, Ohio, and London, England

Copyright © 1987 by The Kent State University Press, Kent, Ohio 44242
All rights reserved
Library of Congress Catalog Card Number 87-2065
ISBN 0-87338-338-9
Manufactured in the United States of America

Radio broadcast of "The Benchbook" is made possible in part through the assistance of the Trial Lawyers Association of America and the Sterling Smith Charitable Trust, H. W. Kane and Ron Wilson, Trustees.

The paper in this book meets the guidelines for permanence and durability of the Committee on Production Guidelines for Book Longevity of the Council on Library Resources.

Library of Congress Cataloging-in-Publication Data

Hayes, Jerry L.
    The benchbook : anecdotes from the lighter side of
the law.

    1. Justice, Administration of—United States—
Anecdotes, facetiae, satire, etc.   2. Justice,
Administration of—Great Britain—Anecdotes,
facetiae, satire, etc.   I. Title.
K184.H39   1987   347'.002'02   87-2065
                          342.700202
ISBN 0-87338-338-9 (alk. paper)

British Library Cataloguing in Publication data are available.

Contents

Foreword

The law closely intertwines with (some would say strangles) our lives. We decry it as ponderous and unduly technical, outrageously expensive, and at times unintelligible, and yet it remains the necessity of our precious free society. As we see a world around us in turmoil with disputes settled by force on the streets or by harsh central authority operating in non-public tribunals we thank our good fortune that the rule of law prevails.

When we examine closely our rule of law we find a quite sensible explanation for much of it— based upon centuries of experience and tradition. Indeed, a close study of the law reveals a colorful tapestry of historical strands.

Judge Jerry L. Hayes of Ohio has conducted such an examination and reports to us with wit and conciseness the origins and explanation of our rule of law. Judge Hayes presents his report in non-legalese and with engaging style so both the lawyer and the layperson may enjoy and learn. Would that we had more such chroniclers of the law instead of the official law journalists and reviewers! For the law to serve most effectively the needs of our free society it must be understood, and Judge Hayes has done an admirable job in making the law more understandable and hence more credible to the average citizen.

It is a pleasure to read his readable text; it is a privilege to recommend such pleasurable and informative reading to the reading public.

Judge John W. Kern III
Dean, The National Judicial College
Reno, Nevada

Preface

William Rogers once said, "The minute you read something you can't understand, you can almost be sure it was drawn up by a lawyer." Well, it's too bad Will Rogers can't hear or read "The Benchbook."

Unfortunately, Rogers's opinion is a common one and in the minds of many the law is drab and boring and colorless. But the image is not the reality. The law lives and its life is filled with romance and excitement and humor. As a lawyer and a judge, I'm proud of my profession and the purpose of "The Benchbook" is to share the fascinating ancestry of the law with you.

WKSU began broadcast of "The Benchbook" in 1983 and syndicated the program for National Public Radio affiliates a year later.

Each episode of "The Benchbook" tells an anecdote of legal history or explains the how and why of one of today's laws. Occasionally, the program takes a whimsical look at the law with such features as The Great Turkey Laws, The Color of Law, and Jerry the Judge's Annual Super Bowl Legal Picks. The goal is to entertain as well as inform and each presentation is made in language a layperson can understand and, hopefully, with some humor. Judging from listener response and from the awards received, it is successful.

Many thanks go to WKSU General Manager John Perry for his willingness to experiment with "The Benchbook," to Executive Producer Mike Flaster for making the program a quality production, to Nancy Graham for the hours of typing and retyping, to Pat Pekar for her research assistance, and to the librarians of America, particularly those of Kent State University, for their aid and assistance. Thanks also go to all the folks at the Kent State University Press for their enthusiasm and assistance in the preparation of this publication.

Because I am so proud of my profession, I am disturbed by the low esteem in which some folks hold the law. My hope is that "The Benchbook," through its radio network and through this printed work will help improve the public understanding and appreciation of the law.

I think you'll enjoy this book and I hope it serves as a reminder that the law is alive and well and living on the airwaves of Public Radio and in the pages of *The Benchbook*.

Introduction:
The Color of Law

Doctors may have an occasional case of scarlet fever or pink eye to cure, but when it comes to color, their diseases pale in comparison to the colors of the law.

I overheard a couple of lawyers arguing about whether or not a school official had "acted under color of law." The student had been dismissed, so the color of law question raised an important legal point. If the official "acted under color of law," he appeared to be acting with legal authority. That appearance of authority would give the student certain legal protections, such as the constitutional right to due process, the right to be told what he did wrong, and the right to a hearing before an impartial judge.

It was an interesting point, and since I didn't know just what color law is really supposed to be, a little research seemed in order. Back in chambers I reached for the law dictionary—appropriately titled *Black's Law Dictionary*—and started to check on the color of law.

Now sometimes the practice of law can be a little boring, but no one should ever say that laws are not colorful. Doctors may have yellow jaundice and black lung disease to work with, or an occasional case of scarlet fever or pink eye to cure. But when it comes to color, their diseases pale in comparison to the colors of the law.

The lawyers have yellow dog contracts and lemon laws, green river ordinances, brown decrees, a silver platter doctrine, gold acts, and scarlet lady laws. They work with red letter law, black letter law, collect black rents and white rents, deal with the problems of white slaves, white acre, whitecaps, and white collar crimes. Of course, there are also the black and tan regulations, the red book of the exchequer, and those all time favorites called blue laws and blue-sky laws. Then, too, students of the law study in such places as Gray's Inn.

The green river ordinances keep unwanted peddlers from your doorstep unless they're invited or have a license. They get their name from Green River, Wyoming, where the town cops arrested the Fuller Brush man for soliciting without an invitation. Blue laws regulate Sunday sales and are a gift from the Puritans of colonial New England. Blue-sky laws regulate stock and security sales. They're called blue-sky laws because some stocks and bonds are so speculative they're about as solid as so many feet of blue sky.

Black rents in Old English law referred to rent paid with work or food as opposed to white rents, which were paid in money or silver. Lemon laws are consumer protection acts and are often aimed at auto sales. Yellow dog contracts were used to force employees to pledge they would not join a union, and a brown decree ends a marriage without saying who was at fault. Whitecap laws prosecute criminal conspiracies and are named after a group of Tennessee outlaws; the ex-chequer's red book was an ancient record of English landholders.

I should also mention the sunshine and sunset laws. Of course, sunshine and sunsets are not colors, but they do conjure up an imaginary array of gorgeous hues. The sunshine laws were passed to make sure public bodies held open meetings so people would know what action was taken and why. And the sunset laws were passed to phase out agencies whose work is no longer necessary.

Well, my research didn't tell me the color of law, and my conclusion is what you've known all along—law, like love, is a many splendored thing.

The How and Why of the Jury System

If you've ever had a chance to serve on a jury, you've been part of a special legal process that people in most other countries don't have or understand.

American jurists thought they had a new idea in 1972 when the one day, one trial jury system was instituted in Houston, Texas. Jurors not picked the first day were finished and those who did land a jury seat were finished at the end of one trial. That was definitely a good idea—it just wasn't new. The Greeks used the same system 2,500 years ago! In fact, they went one step further and guaranteed no trial would last more than one day.

The ancient Greeks loved a good lawsuit. They were even more litigious than twentieth-century Americans, and each year thousands of Greek citizens volunteered for jury duty. Going to court became the national pastime.

Our modern juries of eight or twelve people are puny in comparison to the jury trials held in the world's birthplace of democracy. Hundreds, sometimes thousands, served on a Greek jury. And when the citizens arrived for their jury service, they brought a marble or seashell along to vote with at the end of the trial.

Given this great love for jury trials, the Greeks had to organize their legal system to make sure all litigants got their day in court. But it was to be only one day. All trials—no matter how important—were to begin and end the same day.

Now the ancient Greeks weren't burdened with any formal rules of evidence. The several hundred jurors were seated, the clerk read the complaint, and the parties made speeches. But to complete the trial in one day, some restrictions were needed, so one juror was picked to be timekeeper. His job was to supervise the clepsydra or water clock. A large bucket or pot with a plugged hole was filled with water. When the plaintiff or prosecutor began to speak, the plug was pulled. When the bucket ran out of water, the speaker ran out of time. As soon as the speakers finished, the jury voted. Each juror marched past two large urns and dropped in his marble or seashell for the speaker he thought best.

In a criminal case, the jury also decided the penalty. The prosecutor would make a recommendation; then the defendant would make a recommendation. The jury couldn't change either recommendation, but had to choose which penalty to impose.

For the trial of the famous philosopher Socrates 501 citizen-jurors were assembled. We know today that Socrates was an intellectual giant. Unfortunately, he was not a likeable fellow, and had he been a guest at your party, you might have been inclined to serve him hemlock. He took great delight in showing his brilliance at the expense of others and was condescending with most people. So the citizen-jurors convicted Socrates of impiety, and the prosecutors recommended death. Socrates, on the other hand, suggested he be given free meals for life as a penalty. In a way, Socrates' recommendation was accepted. The jurors agreed to feed him for life; they just decided not to let him live very long. He would have been poisoned immediately, but a religious holiday postponed his execution for thirty days.

Of course, all legal systems have problems—and the Greeks had their share. Due process was a little scarce and some suggest that trials were limited to one day so jurors couldn't be bribed. The Greeks also had problems with the water clocks. Occasionally an unscrupulous character would put mud in the clock's water to stuff up the hole and give one side longer to speak. Society has always had corruption, but as Samuel Johnson said, "It's better to suffer wrong than to do it; and happier to be sometimes cheated than never to trust."

If you've ever had a chance to serve on a jury, you've been part of a special legal process that people in most other countries don't have or understand. The idea for our jury setup began in England about eight hundred years ago. Henry II, the great-grandson of William the Conqueror, was king of the realm and wanted to make his mark on history. You may think you don't know Henry II. Let me suggest you really do, but that you'll recognize him better as Peter O'Toole, who played Henry II in the movie *Beckett*, opposite Richard Burton.

King Henry decided to reform his country's hodgepodge legal system. When he was crowned in 1154 the legal system was a mess. What they did in Lancaster they did differently in Manchester and still differently in London. There was no common law in the country, so Henry set out to make the law, especially the criminal law, the same throughout the realm. To that end he appointed a group of itinerant judges to travel about the land so that the same judges would hear all the cases.

That was a good idea, but as the judges traveled from county to county, they were faced with another problem. Because they didn't live in the areas where they served, they had no idea who had broken the king's law, so there were no defendants. To solve that problem, the judges commanded the leading citizens of each county or shire to present a list of those who had violated the king's peace. The idea was that these people would know all the facts because they lived in the area.

But before these citizens could accuse someone of a crime, they had to take an oath to be truthful. Henry II was of Norman French ancestry and the Norman French word for oath taking was *jurer*, meaning to swear. Thus the group taking the oath came to be called the jury.

Usually about twenty-five people served on those early juries, and their job was simply to present the accused to the court. The issue of guilt or innocence was decided in a trial by battle or ordeal in which God was the final juror. But later, as society became more civilized, a second, smaller group of citizens— usually twelve—began to decide whether or not the accused was guilty. Quite often the jury of twelve was picked from the jury of twenty-five and some folks thought that wasn't quite fair. When the jury of twenty-five met to present the accused only a majority vote was needed. To be fair, it was decided that when the jury of twelve met to determine guilt or innocence a unanimous vote would be needed.

There were, then, big juries and little juries. In English that doesn't sound very sophisticated, but the legal language was Norman French. So there were Le Grand Jury to present the accused and Le Petit Jury or Petits Jurys to determine guilt—a system still with us.

Today defense lawyers scream if the local press or radio tells its audience some important fact about a pending trial, and sometimes trials are moved to a distant city to make sure the jurors do not know what happened until they hear it in the courtroom. Strange, isn't it, that the first jurors were picked specifically because they knew all the facts, while now we spend days picking jurors who know none of the facts.

If you heard a lawyer talking about a Texas Firecracker, you probably wouldn't think he was describing a jury system. But the Texas Firecracker is one of several ideas for improving the American jury.

When called upon most people accept it as

their duty to serve on a jury, but not many actually look forward to the prospect. Jury duty can tie you up for weeks—even months—cause you to lose income, and sometimes even your job. Sure, it's an important part of the judicial system, but it's also a pain.

The first juries were developed in Greece, a nation often called the cradle of democracy. Several hundred years before the birth of Christ, the Greeks were selecting citizens to serve as jurors. Each year six thousand names were pulled. The citizens were divided into smaller groups, called decuries, and then sent out for trial service. Ancient Greek juries numbered in the hundreds—a sort of organized mob rule. A jury of 501 citizens heard the case against Socrates and by a vote of 280 to 221 sentenced him to death.

American juries are a refinement of the British common law jury system—which in turn refined German, French, and Roman jury practice. And since the only thing constant is change, the American system has also been modified over the years. There are three steps in the jury selection process. The first is the making of a list of eligible jurors, called the master wheel. Names are then drawn from the eligible list to form a jury panel; finally, there's the voir dire, or individual questioning of jurors by the judge or lawyers.

In most states your name gets in the master wheel when you register to vote. Then, like a lottery, names are drawn and put into a jury pool to be used when needed. Unfortunately, over 30 percent of Americans eligible to vote fail to register. Some specifically skip registration to avoid jury duty and questions have been raised whether voter lists really provide representative juries. Several states supplement voter lists with names from driver licenses, telephone listings, and welfare and tax roles. This creates a larger and more representative jury pool.

If your name were drawn in the state lottery you would win money; but having your name pulled for jury duty usually costs you both money and time. Most states pay jurors only ten to fifteen dollars a day and employers don't always pay full salaries while their employees serve.

The feeling of fair play is the key to holding public confidence in the legal system and fair play means representative juries. To improve the jury system, some serious reforms have been made. Dozens of court systems, including some federal jurisdictions, adopted the one day, one trial jury program. At the end of one day or the finish of one trial, the juror is excused.

The Texas judiciary adopted a version of that plan called the Texas Firecracker. Jurors are called in for a specific trial. If not selected they can leave immediately and their term is over. It's also cost efficient so Texas gets "the most bang for its buck."

You can help improve the jury system by urging the political leaders of your state to make the jury pools as large and representative as possible and by urging judges to adopt such jury programs as the one day, one trial plan. And finally, when your name is drawn, accept the responsibility. It's a challenge and an adventure and once you've served you'll be glad you did.

Do you know what Jimmy Hoffa, the Archbishop of Canterbury, and the founder of Murder Incorporated have in common? You probably suspect there's very little that trio would share—certainly not the same moral philosophy. But all three did share a common belief in their right not to testify against themselves.

Each in his own time took what we today refer to as the Fifth Amendment. William Samcroft, Archbishop of Canterbury, asserted his right against self-incrimination in 1688—nearly one hundred years before the birth of the American democracy. The archbishop's brush with the criminal law is reported in the "Trial of the Seven Bishops," a fascinating episode in English legal history. It seems that the archbishop and six other leading bishops of the Church of England presented King James II with a written petition suggesting that the king's proclamation about religious freedom was illegal. James II was a Catholic and decided that certain practices of religious discrimination should end. Most agreed with the intent but argued that the king lacked authority to issue the proclamation. The fear was that kings with that sort of power could take as well as give.

The early kings of England were not known for their liberalism, and James II, who was both King of England and Head of the English Church, did not take kindly to the bishop's petition. "Treason," James roared, and he summoned the seven bishops along with their attorneys to appear and answer charges before the King's Court.

When the bishops gathered before the king, the chancellor asked the archbishop if, indeed, he had prepared the petition. Samcroft replied that since he was now an accused criminal he would respectfully decline to say anything which might be incriminating. The king became furious and locked the seven bishops in the Tower of London and ordered them to stand trial. The sight of the leading bishops of the Church of England being paraded off to prison was upsetting and confusing to the people. Even the Tower guards asked the blessing of their prisoners.

A jury of twelve was seated and, after much embarrassment for both church and crown, the trial began. With much difficulty, the crown counsel proved that the bishop and his colleagues did, in fact, prepare the scandalous petition. After several days of the trial, when the jury finally retired to consider its verdict, the nation was near revolution.

The twelve jurors were locked in a room under heavy guard. It was late in the evening when they began deliberations, and they were to have neither food nor water until they reached a decision. At about 4 A.M., some basins of water were delivered so that the jurors might wash, but as thirsty as they were, the water quickly disappeared.

The vote was stalemated at eleven to one for acquittal with Michael Arnold the holdout.

Arnold was the king's brewmeister and was truly behind the eight ball. If he voted not guilty, he could no longer brew beer for the king. But if he voted guilty, he would no longer brew for anyone else. No matter what, he was half-ruined.

Finally, the verdict came in. "Not guilty," said the jury. The crowds cheered, cannons were fired, the king sulked, and poor Arnold, the brewer, went looking for a new job. An interesting example of a beginning step for what was later to become an important American legal principle.

The three words, "If not, not," may lack the magic of "I love you," but they do conjure an image of romance and excitement in the minds of some. "If not, not" has come to stand for the legendary oath of the Aragon people to their king.

History has it that this unique oath began with the words, "We who are as worthy as you," and ended with, "If not, not." In between, the people pledged loyalty to their sovereign as long as he followed the constitution and the law and, "If not, not."

Historically, oaths have played an important role in the story of civilization and the development of a system of law. Even today, the first thing trial witnesses must do is take an oath to "tell the truth, the whole truth, and nothing but the truth," so help them God.

While the oath is important in the modern trial, the oath sometimes *was* the trial in an-

cient Roman and British law. Calling God as a witness to the truth of a claim was so awesome that just the taking of such an oath often ended the trial and the plaintiff won!

As time passed, the judges and juries of yesterday's courts decided the oath of the plaintiff alone was not enough. So, plaintiffs began to bring "oath helpers" with them to court. This method was called trial by compurgation, which means to clear or to purge. The oath helpers would clear a criminal or validate a claim by swearing to their belief in the honesty of the party.

Say that A owes B money. The plaintiff, B, would bring ten men to court. Five would be placed on one side of the room and five on the other. A knife would be tossed in the air. The five to whom the handle pointed were dismissed. One of the other five was removed, and the four left took an oath saying the plaintiff was a truthful and honest person—sort of thirteenth-century character witnesses.

Later the defendants began to take an oath swearing they were right and the other party wrong, and trials turned into swearing contests. If ten men swore for the plaintiff, the defendant might bring in twelve to swear for him; the side having the most "oath helpers" would win.

Eventually the oath helpers began to swear to the facts of the case as well as to the truthfulness of the plaintiff or defendant. For instance, one would swear that he knew Randolph owned Whitacre because the oath helper had been present when the property was given to Randolph. To make sure the testimony of the oath helpers was as fair and accurate as possible, a set of rules—called rules of evidence—was created.

The trial oath of today seems a little shopworn. In fact, trial judges tell juries that they need not believe someone's testimony just because it is given under oath. But the penalties for giving false testimony under oath have always been severe. Today perjury carries a stiff jail term for those convicted. You may remember a fellow named Alger Hiss who went to jail, not because of his Communist connections, but because he lied under oath during a congressional investigation.

So, never take an oath for granted. Swearing a false oath places your liberty at risk and chips away at the foundation of our democracy. Like the good citizens of Aragon, you're entitled to the protection of your government so long as you obey the law and respect the rights of others. But, "If not, not!"

If the dope peddlers of America think the acquittal of John DeLorean in August 1984 means the legal system has taken a kindly attitude toward drug trafficking, they just don't understand the tradition of American and English juries. DeLorean's red-faced prosecutor said the jury had spoken, but the question remains, "What did the jury say?"

Most agree there was enough evidence for a finding of guilty. The concensus seems to be that jurors were so disgusted with the seamy acts of all parties they said, "A pox on both your houses!"

Some point to the DeLorean verdict as an abuse of jury power. Jurors swear to follow the evidence, decide the facts, and then apply the law. Legalists argue that it is not the jury's job to reprimand the government. Fortunately, however, juries have been doing exactly that for centuries. And often at great risk to their own comfort, safety, and personal liberty.

There are countless examples of American and English juries using the verdict to censor a government or king. In 1688, the Archbishop of Canterbury and six other bishops stood before an English jury charged with treason. The bishops had quarreled with the king and issued a proclamation challenging the king's authority. The outraged king sent them to the Tower of London to await the trial. The evidence of the bishops' challenge was clear, but the jury ignored the wishes of the king and set the bishops free.

The most courageous story of jury independence is told in the seventeenth-century trial of William Penn. The famous English Quaker was a constant aggravation to Charles II, and when the king could stand it no longer, he had Penn arrested and charged with the criminal act of preaching to an unlawful assembly. A jury was summoned and ordered by the court to convict him. Penn admitted that he had preached to an assembly in Grace-Church Street but protested that his actions were not unlawful!

The jury quickly found Penn "guilty of preaching in Grace-Church Street," but refused to add the words "to an unlawful assembly."

The angry judge rejected the verdict. The bailiffs were ordered to lock the jury up for the night without so much as a chamber pot. For two days and nights the jury was badgered by the bailiffs and threatened with torture by the judge. They were held in a room without meat, drink, fire, or tobacco and told by the court that they must return a "proper" verdict or starve. Finally, the jury relented, and a new verdict was presented to the court. "Not guilty," said the jury. The verdict earned the jurors the everlasting esteem of Englishmen, but also brought them a fine and jail term from the king.

Following the verdict the judge expressed regret that the jurors had followed their own judgment and opinion rather than the good advice given by the court. But, thank God, both American and English jurors have maintained that independence and continued to follow their own sense of justice.

William Penn, of course, continued aggravating the king and within a few months was arrested again. Eventually, Penn took his Quaker principles across the pond to the American colonies where he founded the great Pennsylvania Commonwealth.

John DeLorean has little in common with William Penn or the Archbishop of Canterbury. But the issue is not John DeLorean but the jury. Those who say the DeLorean jury failed have not done their homework. The DeLorean verdict was just one more example of a jury saying that the king can—and often does—do wrong.

The Courts Yesterday and Today

All of George Washington's appointments to the Supreme Court were lawyers. No president has ever departed from that precedent, but there's no requirement that a justice of the Supreme Court be a lawyer.

Not too many years ago the local cinema was playing a movie called *Star Chamber*. At first, one might think it was a science fiction off-shoot of *Stars Wars*, with spaceships and laser swords. The *Star Chamber*, however, was a melodrama about a group of judges who became disenchanted with the system and put together their own private court, complete with a staff executioner. The title *Star Chamber* was aptly taken from a place in legal history where the Court of the Star Chamber earned a reputation as an evil, vicious, and sinister court.

A witness, as well as the accused, might return home from a session of the Star Chamber with his nose split, his cheeks branded, or his ears stuffed in his back pockets. The good news from a Star Chamber visit was that you couldn't get a death sentence. The bad news was that the judge could, and often did, do just about anything else.

The Court of the Star Chamber got its name from the room where it held its sessions at the Old Palace of Westminster. The King's Council used a chamber that had a ceiling studded with gold stars. The council sometimes sat as a judicial body and eventually the judicial proceedings were called the Court of the Star Chamber.

Frederic W. Maitland, a leading legal historian, describes the court as "a whipping, nose-splitting, ear-cropping court with a grim, unseemly humor of its own." Punishments from the Star Chamber included huge fines, sometimes as much as five thousand pounds, as well as pillory, jail, branding, and mutilation. Torture was a tool used by the court to get the "truth" from witnesses as the court thought "truth" should be.

The Star Chamber trial of William Prynne, a seventeenth-century writer, gives us an example of the court in action. It seems Prynne had written a book which offended the establishment. He was convicted with dispatch in the Star Chamber and sentenced to stand two days in the pillory, a wooden harness device with holes cut in it for the head and wrists. During the course of each day in the pillory, one ear was cut off.

Apparently, Prynne was a slow learner for in a short time he was before the Star Chamber again. This time Prynne had written that one Archbishop Laud was the Arch Agent of the Devil. Well, it was back to the pillory, but, since he had no more ears to cut off, Prynne was branded on both cheeks.

There is, nevertheless, a Cinderella ending to that story. As time passed, the friends of Prynne came into power. Prynne became a hero and was named to Parliament. Archbishop Laud was charged with high treason and another English Court cut off his ears, but they were cut from the neck up. So much for political intrigue in Old England.

It is an ill wind that blows all bad, and there are some good things to be said for the Court of the Star Chamber. When the court first became active, there was much corruption and lawlessness in the realm. The court did clean things up. The Star Chamber Court also was able to hear and punish a series of misdemeanor crimes that the Common Pleas courts could not handle—such crimes as forgery, riot, conspiracy, libel, and one crime dubbed "entangling young gentlemen into contracts of marriage to their utter ruin."

The Court of the Star Chamber was abolished by Charles I in 1614. Some historians have referred to the Star Chamber as an efficient and popular court—obviously those folks were never summoned to appear there. At any rate, it's gone. Let's hope its only return is in the movie.

Making a court appearance has never been a popular American activity. And once in court, people are normally a little nervous, but almost never happy about being there. Still, most judges are nice people, and I wonder just what it is about the judicial image that creates this anxiety. Perhaps it's the lack of pomp and circumstance, or maybe our courts are just not colorful or creative enough.

American courts pale by comparison with their English counterparts. Our judges sit in little drab courtrooms wearing gloomy black robes, whereas our legal ancestors were trumpeted into colorful chambers wearing powdered wigs, silk scarves, and red velvet robes. Even the names of our courts seem dull by comparison. In the United States, we have district courts, common pleas courts, superior courts, and municipal courts. But how much more exciting it might be if we were subpoenaed to appear before the Court of Wards and Liveries or to be ordered to appear before the Verder of the Court of Swainmoat and Attachment of the New Forest.

The predecessors to the twentieth-century courts of modern America reflect the majesty, splendor, and some of the more colorful customs of the local communities in our English legal heritage. We find reports of trials held in the Bristol Tolzey Court, the Liverpool Court of Passage, the Salford Hundred Court, the Court of Arches, the Court of the Forest, and an interesting little Court of Limited Jurisdiction which became affectionately known as the Pie Powder Court.

The Pie Powder Courts were found at the market fairs held throughout Great Britain. The name is a corruption of the Norman French words *Pied Poudre*, which literally mean dusty feet. The Pie Powder Court or the Court of the Dusty Feet was so-called because of the dusty feet of the traveling merchants who appeared as litigants and because the judges sat on a bench close to the ground and often had dirty shoes. The Pie Powder Court was a court of the marketplace where merchants could have a quick hearing to settle their disputes. Much of modern commercial law was born in the decisions of Pie Powder Court justices.

In American courts we have judges and clerks and bailiffs. But in Old England a judge was more than just a judge. The judge of the Liverpool Court of Passage, for instance, also held the title of Moss Reever and Burliman. In addition, he was the Registrar of Leather Sealers, the Scavenger, the Alefounder or Taster, and Fryer of Seized Leather. As Moss Reever and Burliman, his job was to protect the queen's liege or the river people from being aggrieved by any outside fishermen. As Scavenger, he was responsible for saving the folks from any annoyance from peddlers' carts. As Alefounder, it was up to him to make sure that the local brewers put out a good beer and that the bakers fed the citizens properly. As the Fryer of Seized Leather, he was to make sure that shoes seized from any of the passing vessels were well made and serviceable. All this he was to do to the best of his skill and judgment "so help him God."

The next time you find yourself in a court, you might address the judge as His Excellency the Scavenger, or ask him how the Alefounder's business is, or check into how the queen's liege is holding up. If the judge is a history buff or fan of "The Benchbook," he will give you a knowledgeable smile. But if he looks a bit startled, you'd probably better keep quiet and move along as quickly as possible.

The first Monday in October is traditionally the season kick off for the United States Su-

Kick off for the Supreme Court

preme Court. For the court's nine justices, the first Monday is the beginning of the new October term. With some pomp and circumstance they don their black robes, pause to shake hands, and then enter the imposing marble courtroom to begin another year's work.

As kids we were told about the three separate but equal branches of the government. But like the animals of Orwell's farm, some seem more equal than others. Critics argue the modern court has become the supreme branch of government and everyone agrees its power is awesome. But it wasn't always that way; the court's beginnings were really quite humble.

President Washington created the court with the Judiciary Act of 1789 and its membership was set at six. Of Washington's first six nominations to the court, one refused, one accepted but never attended, and John Jay, the first chief justice, spent most of his tenure in Europe as a diplomat. In fact, Chief Justice Jay resigned to become governor of New York and when later was asked to return as chief justice, he refused saying he didn't think the court would ever amount to much.

By the late twentieth century annual requests for hearings numbered in the thousands. But business was slow in the beginning and Jay's frustration is understandable. The first case didn't even get to court until 1791 and the court was three years old before it issued its first opinion. The justices earned their princely $3,500 annual salary, traveling about the country to preside over the circuit courts.

All of George Washington's appointments to the Supreme Court were lawyers. No president has ever departed from that precedent, but there's no requirement that a justice of the Supreme Court be a lawyer, nor is there any requirement that the justices be American born. In fact, six Supreme Court justices were born outside the United States.

Over the years, the number of justices changed with the political winds and FDR's "Court Picking Plan" of 1936 was far from a new idea. Originally set at six justices, the number went to five, back to six, to seven, and then to nine. The peak was reached in 1863 when there were ten justices, but in 1866 the number went back to seven. In 1869 Congress said that the Supreme Court shall consist of a chief justice of the United States and eight associate justices and the number has held at nine ever since.

Some of the more famous names of modern society have come to us with compliments of the court. We all know the name Miranda, and the courts of yesteryear gave us Dred Scott, Marbury, Korematsu, Mapp, Terry, Gideon, Brown, and Sullivan to pick just a few from a long list.

Of course, debate over the court's power will be with us for years to come. But it's hard to imagine nine people in black robes representing a serious threat. The court commands no army, has a total staff of about three hundred, and spends less than fifteen million dollars a year. In today's world of megabuck budgets, the Supreme Court is a modest operation, but essential to a free society. Chief Justice Taney in 1859 said, "As long as the Constitution exists, the Court must exist with it to decide in a peaceful forum the angry . . . controversies . . . that in other countries have been determined by force." Like all courts, it will function only so long as it maintains the confidence and respect of the people it serves.

If you tell a cabbie in Washington, D.C. to take you up to "The Hill," you'll get a ride to Capitol Hill. That's where the power brokers meet to chart the course of government, and it's the home of our Congress. But behind the Capitol itself, there's a white marble building that's the home of the United States Supreme Court and the mecca of the American legal community.

To some it's a beautiful building; to others it's a white elephant. It's been called a marble palace and a marble mausoleum, and at the court's first session, one justice said the members of the court looked like "nine black beetles in the Temple of Karnak." But for the first 145 years of the court's existence, it was a vagabond group moving from city to city, place to place. Some of its early quarters have been called "mean and dingy" and "little better than a dungeon."

The court had always met in the nation's capital, so the first session in 1790 was held at the Royal Exchange Building in New York City. Only three of the six justices showed up and, even though one was wearing a grand new judicial wig, the session was cancelled since it lacked a quorum.

By the end of the court's second term, Congress had moved the capital to Philadelphia where the justices shared a courtroom with the Philadelphia mayor's court. Unfortunately for the Supreme Court justices, the mayor's court was busy while the Supreme Court had no cases to hear. So, the mayor kicked the Supreme Court out. Although the Supreme Court had no cases scheduled in its early days, the justices were required to travel the country as circuit judges and were kept busy hearing federal cases out on the stump for the first century of the court's existence.

In January 1801, the capital moved to Washington, D.C. and the Supreme Court was again without a home. The commissioners of Washington finally gave the court permission to hold sessions in a first-floor room of the Capitol. Later, it met in an old library of the House of Representatives. But a favorite meeting place of the court was "Long's Tavern." The tavern was the scene of the nation's first Inaugural Ball and is where the Library of Congress now stands.

In 1810, the court returned to the Capitol and met in the basement beneath the Senate chamber. It stayed there until the British burned the building in 1814. In fact, legend has it that Supreme Court documents were used to start the fire.

Around 1912, President Taft began promoting the idea of a special building just for the court. Taft, incidentally, is the only American to serve both as president and as chief justice of the Supreme Court. Anyway, on October 7, 1935, 145 years after it first met in

New York and 134 years after it moved to Washington, the nation's highest tribunal got a home of its own. The site for the court's new home was the old "Brick Capitol" area used by Congress when the British burned the original Capitol.

The amount authorized for construction was $9,740,000, more than $3 million of which was spent for marble. Congress expected a call for more money to furnish court quarters. But the building was finished and furnished with money to spare. The replacement cost is today pegged at over $100 million, making the court building a good buy and a good investment. And, if you forgive a biased opinion, it's another example of the fact that the judiciary has always been the bargain branch of the American democracy.

The New Deal and the Nine Old Men, the Sick Chicken Case, and a Switch in Time that saved Nine—some newspaper headlines from the pages of yesterday's press that fit together to tell an interesting story of the courts and the law.

But, before we slip into the legal henhouse which hatched our drama, let me describe the times. The Crash of 1929 shook the foundations of most American institutions. Banks, the stock market, businesses, and industries were all in trouble. Even the courts were shaken, including our Supreme Court.

Between September 1, 1929 and July 1, 1932 the value of stocks on the New York Ex-

change fell $74 billion. Unemployment, bankruptcy, and economic despair brought America to near revolution.

In 1932, a disenchanted people asked Franklin D. Roosevelt to turn the nation around, and in the first 100 days of his presidency, Roosevelt pushed through legislation that was, indeed, revolutionary.

Two of the most important New Deal measures were the Agricultural Adjustment Act, the AAA, and the National Industrial Recovery Act. The NIRA established codes for fair competition, including wage and hour regulations and working condition requirements.

The business community was furious with the alphabet soup agencies of the New Deal and their power to rule and regulate. "Take the battle to the courts" became the war cry, and the legality of New Deal legislations was soon challenged. Finally, in what's now called the Sick Chicken Case, the egg was laid on the doorstep of the U.S. Supreme Court.

The Sick Chicken Case is really the *Schechter Poultry Corporation v. U.S.* The Schechter people operated a New York City poultry slaughter house and they were indicted for eighteen counts of violating the Live Poultry Code. This was an administrative code OK'd by Roosevelt and the NIRA. The wage and hour regulations apparently crimped Schechter's business style.

Schechter turned to the legal system for help and claimed the act was an unconstitutional delegation of power. The nine justices of the

Supreme Court agreed and struck down the act, dealing the New Deal a bad blow. Roosevelt was furious. The justices, six of whom were over 70, were called the Nine Old Men, and the president said he wanted a Supreme Court which would "do justice under the Constitution, not over it."

The electorate responded. In 1936, Roosevelt was reelected by an overwhelming margin, and he quickly proposed legislation which would permit the appointment of an additional Supreme Court justice for each one over 70 who had not retired. The proposal was referred to as Roosevelt's Court Packing Plan, and cries of outrage came from the minority side. But strong voices of approval were heard from the people and the New Deal politicians.

Then, on March 29, 1937, before Congress could act on the Court Packing Plan, the Supreme Court decided another New Deal case involving the National Industrial Recovery Act. Justice Roberts, who had helped provide a five to four majority for the conservatives, switched his vote and the NIRA legislation was declared constitutional. The vote of Justice Roberts was referred to as "a switch in time that saved nine" and provided Roosevelt's New Deal with new life.

The Court Packing Plan, an egg laid by the Sick Chicken Case, never hatched and the Supreme Court remains today a body of nine—although the justices will probably never again be referred to as the nine old men.

Colorful Magistrates and Their Work

American frontier justice may have been a little rough around the edges, but for the most part the people involved were decent folks who simply saw their duty and then they done it!

n the late 1800s, people used to say there was no law west of the Pecos. But that, of course, was before the Honorable Roy Bean opened his combination courthouse and saloon in the West Texas town of Vinegaroon. The colorful sign outside that small wooden building proclaimed it the headquarters of Judge Roy Bean, Notary Public, Justice of the Peace, and "All the Law West of the Pecos."

A storehouse of colorful tales is part of our legacy from that famous old frontier oracle. Some have been exaggerated by time; others by Roy Bean himself. But, they make an interesting chapter in our legal heritage.

Bean began his life in the hills of Kentucky around the year 1825 and was a rogue from childhood on. He saw more than one jail from the inside looking out before he went into the judging business. In fact, he was once hanged by the friends of a Mexican he had shot. Fortunately for Bean, the rope stretched enough to keep him alive until his girlfriend cut him down.

After the hanging incident, Bean quickly decided another part of the country would be better for his health, and the next sixteen years he lived a semi-respectable life in San

Antonio, Texas. He married, had children, and sold firewood, which he stole, and milk, which he watered, to make his living. But eventually, he grew tired of respectability. He drifted west, across the Pecos River, where he sold whiskey from a tent to thirsty railroad builders.

Running a frontier saloon was tough work. The saloon keeper was often called on to settle disputes between rough customers. But the tall Roy Bean, with his bushy beard and ready six-shooters, was just the man for the job. In fact, he was so good at settling these disputes that the Texas Rangers, looking for a court to use, decided to have Bean appointed justice of the peace.

So in 1884, Roy Bean began operating his "West of the Pecos Justice Center." Of course, he continued to pour whiskey at the same time. To add dignity to his new court, Judge Bean got a blank book and recorded some of the laws he would enforce. On one page he wrote, "Cheating and horse stealing is hanging offenses if ketched," and on another he penned, "A full beats a straight unless the one holding the full is not straight or is himself too full."

Despite popular belief, Judge Bean never had anyone hanged. He was more interested in the fine money. The Texas attorney general once asked Bean why he didn't send the state its share of the fines. Bean replied that since the state didn't send him any money, he didn't see why he should send any to the state.

Sometimes our British cousins shake their heads at the stories of Judge Bean and look down their noses at the courts of the western frontier. But they forget the English Court of the Star Chamber that slit the noses of British citizens. Judge Roy Bean was a better judge than some of the lord high chancellors of Old England and no American court, even in the Wild West, ever used the rack or thumb screw to interrogate a witness.

American frontier justice may have been a little rough around the edges, but for the most part the people involved were decent folks who simply saw their duty and then they done it!

Most people have heard at least one story about Judge Roy Bean; he was a little high-handed in his courtroom operation and certainly not the sort of judge one would want to fool around with. But Bean wasn't the only judge to run a courtroom with a tight fist.

Another judge in a western mining town once presided at a murder trial at which the defendant was absent. The evidence was presented and the jury came back with a verdict of not guilty. The judge shook his head and said, "Well, I'm going to have to send you back to reconsider your verdict." The jurors weren't dumb and they got the message. Shortly thereafter they came back with a verdict of guilty. The judge said, "That's more like it. After all, we hanged the defendant earlier this morning."

But don't think American Wild West judges were the only ones who badgered jurors. In the thirteenth century when the jury system was just beginning, there was an English judge who wasn't quite sure whether a defendant could be tried by a jury without his consent. He solved the problem by eliminating the trial and hanging everyone accused.

Early British jurors really had tough duty. They were locked in small, stuffy rooms to deliberate and held there without food and water until they reached a verdict. It wasn't necessary then for a verdict to be unanimous. Often, votes came in ten to two or eleven to one. After the court accepted the verdict, holdout jurors were punished. In those days, the judiciary was not an independent body. It was an extension of the king. The judge could make his own determination as to what the verdict should be and a juror could be whipped or fined or sent to prison for failing to vote the proper way.

Englishman Lord Chief Justice George Jeffreys might have written the book for our Judge Bean to follow. Chief Justice Jeffreys has been described by some as the worst judge that ever disgraced Westminster Hall. A prime example of his roughshod tactics and jury badgering is seen in the seventeenth-century trial of the Lady Alice Lisle.

Lady Lisle let two renegade deserters from the English Army into her home. When they came in, she recognized one of them as a rebel and sent her servant to report him to the justice of the peace. But before that could be done, someone else reported their presence and Lady Lisle was arrested for harboring a traitor. Jeffreys wasn't too concerned with whether or not she was guilty and decided to make an example of her. The evidence against Lady Lisle was pretty thin and after badgering the witnesses, the Lord Chief Justice turned his attention to the jury. The charge to the jury would have made a prosecutor proud. They were given a clear understanding that they should find the defendant guilty. They retired, and shortly returned with a verdict of acquittal. The judge was furious and sent them back to reconsider. Three times in all they returned with the same verdict, which the judge refused to accept. Finally, after the judge threatened the jurors with imprisonment if they persisted with such a verdict, they did what the judge wanted and brought in a verdict of guilty. The prisoner was condemned to be burned alive, but on petition to the king her execution was changed to beheading and was so carried out.

Four years later, the conviction of Lady Lisle was repealed on the ground that she had been indicted for entertaining a traitor, knowing him to be such, whereas the said person was not, at that time, convicted of any such crime—not much help to Lady Lisle. In the early days of the jury system, it was not only difficult to be a juror—defendants had a pretty tough time too.

When the crowd at Yankee Stadium roars, "Kill the Umpire," nobody gets too upset. The umpire probably doesn't take it too kindly, but he knows that he'll wake up in the morning safe in his own bed. But when a lynch mob at the turn of the century cried, "Kill somebody," there was plenty to worry about. An accused in the hands of that crowd would be lucky to get off just being tarred and feathered. Death by hanging was the more likely outcome; and between 1882 and 1950, more than five thousand Americans died at the hands of these ugly mobs.

Lynching is one of the few real blots on our legal heritage, and while we often associate this outrage with cowboys and the Wild West, it was really more of a southern invention. To be sure, frontier America had its share of prairie necktie parties, but they were the work of vigilantes in towns and territories without any formal law. Lynching is a gift of a so-called civilized society where the sheriffs and judges simply turned their backs on the shameful actions of lawless mobs.

But as terrible as lynching is, it does an even greater injustice to a Virginia gentleman named Charles Lynch. Lynch was a Quaker by birth, but during the troubled times of the Revolutionary War he felt compelled to accept public office. Taking a public oath, however, violated Quaker beliefs and Lynch found himself at odds with his church. Then, as the battlefields of war moved nearer his home, Lynch reluctantly accepted a commission as colonel in the home guard militia.

Horse stealing was a serious military problem of the times. Tory sympathizers would steal horses and give or sell them to the British armies. Bringing these thieves to justice was next to impossible. The regular felony courts were several hundred miles from Lynch's home guard command. Sending defendants off for trial was usually wasted effort and dangerous for the witnesses. British armies often captured the travelers, and even more often the defendant's Tory friends arranged escapes.

So Colonel Lynch became Judge Lynch when he and three of his neighbors set up their own informal court to try local horse thieves and vandals. Every defendant had a trial. He could face his accuser, cross examine witnesses, and give testimony. If acquitted, he received an apology. If convicted, his punishment was according to the Law of Moses—forty lashes, minus one. Then the thief was told to shout, "Liberty Forever." If he refused, he was strung up by his thumbs until he said the magic words. But, no defendant in Lynch's informal court was ever hanged.

When the war ended, some of these Tory sympathizers threatened to sue Colonel Lynch. So the Virginia legislature passed a law to indemnify Lynch and the members of his court. That legislation became known as Lynch's law and called national attention to the court of Judge Lynch. Because Lynch had used physical punishment on those he convicted, lynching became the term applied to any summary physical punishment without a formal hearing.

So as Greece, the cradle of democracy, gives us the term *Draconian,* the American bastion of liberty and justice gives us the term *lynching.* But Magistrate Draco earned his reputation, while Judge Lynch, the Quaker gentleman from Virginia, did not!

∽

I heard a story at a recent meeting about an old village justice of the peace. The man pictured himself as a great jurist with unlimited jurisdiction, but it seems that he kept a mail-order catalog between the cloth covers of an old lawbook. Once, when an unlucky out of state speeder appeared, the learned jurist put on his glasses, picked up his mail-order lawbook, cleared his throat, and solemnly pronounced a sentence of $29.95. The defendant began to protest that he had never paid more than $20 for a speeding ticket. He was about to continue his protest when the arresting officer whispered, "You better shut up. You're lucky his honor put his finger on pants and not on pianos."

People seem to find that story amusing. It fits the popular image of a backwoods, country justice of the peace, but the popular image doesn't fit the facts. The justice of the peace was an important part of English history for over eight hundred years. The magistrates of Old England, or justices of the peace, were among the most influential men in England during the sixteenth, seventeenth, and eighteenth centuries.

After the Norman conquest of 1066, the new kings appointed "Conservators of the Peace" to watch over their lands. As the years passed, their power grew, and by 1361 they had become so influential that parliament enacted a Justice of the Peace Act giving JP's authority to apprehend, indict, and try criminals, to hold a civil court, and to settle property disputes.

These justices were charged with administering laws and raising soldiers for the king's armies. They had the authority to fine people, to take property, to send people to prison, and, in some cases, even to make prisoners their slaves.

One of history's greatest lawyers, Sir Edward Coke, said that the JP's provided a form of government which ensured the tranquility and quiet of the realm and was a model for the entire Christian world. For all practical purposes, it was the JP's who made local government work in Great Britain, and the justice of the peace was the mainstay in the development of the English judicial system.

With the political and judicial status of the JP's solidified by custom and law in Old England, it was a relatively easy matter to transplant the legal office of justice of the peace to the American colonies. With each new wave of immigrants, the office grew in stature and strength. The notion that the justice of the peace in the United States was uniquely an American institution, completely opposite from the JP in England, is not correct. The justices of the peace helped design and weave together the social and political fabric of America in the same manner as they did in England. The new Americans wanted and needed the JP's to bring law and order to their communities.

The JP's have been regarded by many as an uneducated group of illiterate persons with no legal training and no access to the written law. The facts, however, show that the local JP's were often educated in law and their opinions based on written legal sources. The JP courts have been characterized as dealing primarily with criminals when, in fact, most of their litigation consisted of civil actions.

So, the next time you see Archie Campbell waving his cigar and playing the goofy justice of the peace in *Hee Haw*, it's OK to laugh. But remember, it's about as real as Tarzan, King Kong, or the locust that ate Kansas.

In the summer of 1692, the Puritans of Massachusetts brought the devil to the courtroom. The village of Salem was the legal arena for the trial of Satan's agents. Before the summer had ended, 19 Massachusetts men and women and two dogs were hanged for practicing witchcraft. Another man was crushed to death for standing mute at his trial, 55 confessed that they were witches, and 150 languished in prison. These grim figures record the data of the seventeenth century so-called Salem witch trials—an infamous but fortunately brief period in American legal and social history.

Satan's mark was deeply impressed on the minds of the Puritan Pilgrims. The England they left behind had witnessed witchcraft trials by the score. In fact, from the fourteenth century on, all of Europe had been engaged in a witch-hunting bloodbath.

When the Salem citizens began their war on the witches, they were without a colonial charter of government. By the time the new charter arrived from England, the jails of Sa-

lem were bulging with accused witches. The governor quickly created a special court and appointed seven judges—none of whom had any legal training—to hear the trials. One judge, a Cambridge graduate, took one look at the situation and promptly resigned.

By the seventeenth century, the persecution of witches in England was on the ebb. Still, nearly three hundred years of witchcraft trials provided vivid memories for the New England settlers. King Henry VIII, as head of the Church of England, had made witchcraft a crime punishable by death. But those accused of being witches normally had more to fear from angry citizens than from the law. Witch burning was more often done by a lynch mob. Hundreds were burned as witches because of the ancient superstition that only fire could destroy their power.

It could be dangerous to have a small animal for a pet. An affectionate dog or cat, particularly one trained to perform tricks, could get you charged with witchcraft—especially if you and the neighbors were at odds. In English law, a single witness couldn't convict someone of murder, but one was enough for a conviction of witchcraft.

Unfortunately, things were just as bad in the American colonies. There was a presumption of guilt. An accusation from an angry neighbor or the imagination of a small child was enough to send you to the gallows. In fact, it was the children who started the Salem witchhunt.

The 55 confessed Salem witches did so to

save their lives. Those who pled not guilty ended up on the gallows. Sarah Good, for example. A child accused Sarah, saying she had stabbed her. The child even produced part of the knife. Then a man in the courtroom stood up with the rest of the knife. He said that the knife was his, that he had broken it the day before and thrown away the upper part. But, the facts didn't matter. Sarah Good was declared guilty and hanged on July 19. When she came to the scaffold on Gallows Hill, her minister urged her to confess that she was a witch. "You are lying," she affirmed. "I am no more of a witch than you are wizard, and if you take away my life, God will give you blood to drink." Some years later when the minister died, his throat was filled with blood, fulfilling the Salem prophecy.

There is an old saying that the wheels of justice grind slowly—but they grind exceedingly fine. Often the so-called quibbles of the law serve as our defense against hysteria or mob rule. The presumption of innocence and the prohibition of hearsay evidence are barriers against the tides of suspicion and fear. Salem reminds us that even the well-meaning can commit wholesale crimes against humanity. We need protections against ignorance and malice—protection offered to us today by an active and independent judicial system.

In 197 B.C., the legions of Rome quelled a revolt in Further Spain. But before the soldiers returned home, they took hostages to guarantee the future good conduct of the rebels. Hostages were also taken at the end of the sixteenth-century Irish Rebellion and the eighteenth-century French Counterrevolution. In 1193, the Austrian Duke Leopold kidnapped Richard the Lionhearted for whom he received a fat ransom from the English people. In fact, the word "kidnap" is said to have originated in British harbor towns where thugs stole children to sell into slave labor.

So kidnapping and hostage taking are nothing new. In fact, these tools of the modern terrorist, like terrorism itself, are as old as recorded history. Some say that the roots of terrorism were planted during the Zealot struggle for Palestine chronicled in the first century A.D. In the eleventh century, a Persian and Syrian religious sect called the Assassins added a new weapon to the terrorist arsenal, but the doctrine of terrorism was around for years before the Assassins felled their first victims.

Aristotle and Plato debated the morality of terrorism and so did Cicero and Thomas Aquinas. Human memory may be frail and short, but the question of murder for political and religious purpose has occupied the thoughts and writings of philosophers and theologians for over two thousand years.

So it's no surprise that the ancient traditions of terror are carried on by twentieth-century zealots. Unfortunately, the tools of modern society permit a more vicious and sensational program of fear. So now, every few months, some nation of the so-called civilized world, with all its laws and courts and judges and marshalls, finds itself in the frustrating grip of international terrorism.

Between 1970 and 1979, there were more than 8,000 major terrorist incidents. Over 8,000 people were wounded by terrorists and nearly 4,000 were killed. There were 1,400 assassinations, 536 kidnappings, 4,400 bombings, 89 hijackings, and 2,000 attacks on business, industrial, or military facilities.

And the decade of the eighties is no better. The number of attacks causing death or injury rose from 25 in 1968 to over 200 in 1980, and the number of major terrorist attacks rose from fewer than 200 in 1960 to 800 in 1983.

The violent attacks of the PLO, the IRA, the Japanese Red Army, the Red Brigades, the Baader-Meinhof gang, and the Beirut militia dramatically show how impotent the law can be in dealing with the fanatic. As Christian scriptures suggest, "Those, having not the law, are a law unto themselves!"

But while the law is sometimes a feeble reed, the legal systems of the world are trying to cope with the problem and have increased efforts to curb terrorism. The Tokyo Convention of 1963, the Montreal Convention of 1971, the Organization of American States Convention of 1973, and the European Convention of 1978 are but a few of the more recent attempts of the international community to contain terrorism.

The frustrations surrounding terrorist acts often trigger knee-jerk reactions for a military response. But in the long run, patience may be the most potent weapon and the acts of violence reemphasize the need for accepted rules of law. Dwight Eisenhower once remarked, "The clearest way to show what the rule of law means to us in everyday life is to recall what has happened when there is no law," and Edmund Burke, one of history's greatest patriots and freedom fighters, said, "Our patience will achieve more than our force!"

Every once in a while I hear someone say that the neighbor's kids played havoc with his home. Fortunately, that's never quite true since the term *havoc* is an old military command that means to massacre without quarter. You may remember Shakespeare's line in Julius Caesar, "Cry 'havoc' and let slip the dogs of war." But even in wartime the concept of havoc became so outrageous that King Richard II threatened death to any officer giving the command. And so, *havoc* found a place in the volumes on the laws of war.

It's hard to believe that an uncivilized act like war can be governed by civilized rules. But soldiers and statesmen have devoted time and attention to regulating armed conflict for thousands of years. The warriors of ancient Greece and the legions of old Rome fought under a well-developed law of arms. Before international treaties were signed, the laws of chivalry were well in place, and centuries before Nuremberg sentenced its war criminals, an English court of chivalry was settling disputes among warring knights.

In the late 1300s the English army laid siege

to a French village. "Havoc" was the command. But when three French knights laid down their swords, they called on the British commander to act under the law of arms and accordingly their lives were spared—a fourteenth-century forerunner of the Geneva Convention.

The primary sources for laws of war are custom and treaty, and the best known treaty is the Geneva Convention, which sets rules for prisoners of war. But the first international agreement was the 1856 Paris Declaration on Maritime War. Then came the St. Petersburg Declaration, a dozen different Hague conventions, several Geneva protocols and conventions, the Treaty of Versailles, the Red Cross Rules, the United National Charter, and several U.N. resolutions.

Modern laws of war regulate naval and land war, poison gas and exploding bullets, mine warfare, genocide, care for the wounded, sick and shipwrecked, set rules of conduct for civilians, children, and prisoners, and establish a special protocol for journalists. After all, what good is a war if there's no one to write about it?

Cicero once said, "The laws are silent in time of war," but that seems too pessimistic. Despite weaknesses, the laws of war have influenced the conduct of battle. The ideas that prisoners have a right to live, that children should be spared, that hospitals are not legitimate targets, and that victorious nations get responsibilities as well as rewards involve principles more accepted today than at any other time in history.

The zealots of peace are skeptical of all attempts to regulate war. But Homer's *Iliad* reminds us that "men grow tired of sleep, love, singing and dancing sooner than of war." Even the United Nations charter doesn't forbid the use of force. Realism demands the recognition that war does and probably will happen. That mandates civilized people to do all possible to mitigate war's worst ravages.

Ben Franklin said, "There never was a good war or a bad peace," and President George Washington told Congress in 1790, "To be prepared for war is the most effectual means of preserving the peace." For so-called civilized people, the preparation for war includes adoption of laws providing for the conduct of conflict. It's not an endorsement of war, but simply a belief that standards of civilization exist by which people's conduct can and will be judged.

No chronicle of history's world-class barbarians would be complete without the name of Draco the Magistrate. A barbarian, by definition, is a fierce, brutal, or cruel person. And the name Draco, 2,500 years after the magistrate gave Athens its first set of written laws, is still attached to any law that seems cruel or repressive. Twentieth-century laws with exceptionally harsh penalties are called Draconian. Laws that call for castration of sex offenders, or cutting the hands off thieves, or imprisoning drug users for life are considered Draconian laws.

Draco was appointed magistrate of Athens in

621 B.C., and the code of Draco made death the penalty for crimes both great and small. Even idleness or laziness was a capital crime, and those who stole fruit from the market were punished in the same way as those who murdered or committed sacrilege.

According to legend, Draco wrote his laws in blood, not ink, and when asked why he made death the penalty for nearly all crimes he said, "The lesser ones deserve it, and for the greater no heavier penalty could be found."

Draco's work as a lawgiver is surrounded by some mystery. He was appointed magistrate of Athens shortly after an unsuccessful attempt to overthrow the government of that Greek city-state. But the poor were still oppressed beyond endurance and the city government was forced to make concessions. Draco's laws were a result of those concessions. His legislation restored government to the people, but his constitution was too complex and the laws too severe to win or keep popular support.

But as harsh as the Draconian code was, it was still a step forward, and the seeds of some modern legal principles are found in his code. The germ for the idea of an appellate system is in the Draconian code, and his laws on manslaughter were progressive and relatively mild for the times. But other harsher laws are attributed to Draco—laws which permitted the selling of men into slavery and others which regulated religion and education. Draco is also credited with a law forcing judges to listen to both sides of the case— certainly cruel and unusual punishment for judges.

But even though the Draconian code was an improvement, the harsh penalties did little to comfort the restless citizens of Athens. Reforms were demanded and the next generation brought one of the wisest statesmen and lawgivers of all times to the magistrate's post. Solon was Draco's replacement and Draco's code was destroyed. Only his laws on manslaughter remained for history to examine.

So, in one of life's many paradoxes we find that Greece, the land that gave birth to the first democratic society known to man, the land that gave us Socrates and Aristotle, is also the land that gave us the first set of Draconian laws.

But Magistrate Draco is involved in another of history's paradoxes along with a barbarian found in a neighbor nation to the west. This second barbarian was the Caesar named Caligula, one of Rome's more bloodthirsty emperors. For fun, Caligula posted his decrees on the tops of tall temple columns. Citizens would then unknowingly violate his laws and he would have them "legally" arrested. His early use of the maxim "ignorance of the law is no excuse" cost more than one Roman citizen his head.

But now, the paradox. Draco, the Greek magistrate, and Caligula, the Roman Caesar, are acknowledged barbarians. Yet, the word *barbarian* originally meant foreigner or, more specifically, a person not Greek and not Roman and, therefore, not civilized.

Police, Prisons, and Punishment

At common law, a scold was a troublemaker who spent the day gossiping, spreading rumors, brawling, and being an all around pain in the public peace.

One of the more colorful characters in the history of the English legal system was a chap called a "detection official." He most certainly was a pillar of the Church of England, but with the rest of the community he was about as popular as the plague.

The real title of the detection official was summoner, and he was the medieval equivalent of today's stool pigeon or snitch. The summoner's job was to report to the church wardens those folks he felt were guilty of some moral offense.

Now, before you say, "So what," let me remind you that the Church of England was the country's official religion. The Church and State were not separate. While the State courts were busy punishing crime, the Church courts were even busier punishing sin. For over six hundred years, the Church courts watched and regulated people's morals.

Like modern courts, the Church courts had several levels. At the bottom rung of the ladder was the archdeacon's court. It handled the "common" moral offenses of the day. Chaucer once said the archdeacon's court punished lechery most of all and as a result these courts were known as the bawdy courts.

Every once in a while today we complain that the law gets a bit petty. That's when we get a jay-walking or parking ticket or we're cited for hitchhiking or letting our dog run loose. Well, if you think you've got troubles, look at what you might have been charged with by the Old English detection official.

In 1569, Joan Towler was cited because the congregation was offended by the clothes she wore to Sunday services, Robert Deryck because he set up a maypole in the church-yard, and the wife of Michael Johnson for digging in her garden during evening prayer. John Moore and his wife were charged with not attending church services. Their defense was that they were both too fat to travel—a condition that bawdy court set about to remedy.

For the long-suffering spouses of American golfers, let me tell you your plight is historic. Hugh Radford, among others, was fined for playing golf on Sunday as far back as 1618. Of course, golfers are not the only ones to have played when they should have prayed. In 1575, Robert Fulborne was cited for bowl-ing; John Stewart in 1623 for playing tennis; and in 1600, Michael Anderson decided Sunday football was more fun than church. I guess some things never change. Of course, there were major offenses, too—such things as forgery, adultery, fornication, perjury, and blasphemy.

To make matters worse, these were not just ten dollar and cost cases. Usually the sen-tence involved some form of public punish-ment. In 1639, Susan Semor sat on the stool of repentence—a high chairlike device in a raised box in the center of the church. The entire congregation could then enjoy her humiliation.

Normally, a public confession was made in the town square. Offenders wore white sheets or sackcloth and walked around bare-foot carrying a candle. In 1696, Thomas Heath did public penance after he was found guilty of buying the services of another man's wife and paying for her by the pound.

Fines were sometimes levied and everyone charged had to pay a church fee, like court costs, even if they were found innocent. Whippings, time in the stocks, and, occa-sionally, jail was part of the sentence for sin.

So, next time you find yourself in court, you might suggest to the judge a little public pen-ance for your speeding ticket. But, on second thought, maybe you better just pay the fine and costs.

Law enforcement officials have operated under a dozen different names over the years. They've been called constables, gen-darmes, sheriffs, bobbies, peelers, crushers, and, of course, cops.

Each title has a history. For instance, accord-ing to one school, the term *cop* comes from the British abbreviation for constable on pa-trol. But another school says the title was given to policemen because of the copper badges they wore. Both stories are probably correct. The title constable once meant a high officer of a royal household, but by the time it appeared in the American colonies, the constable's job was left to the poor and was held by local toughs who wanted a little authority. At any rate, these titles are the more modern and familiar ones.

In the history of law enforcement we find some rather interesting obscure titles along with some bizarre duties. Old England gave us the "detection official" who busied himself with punishing sin. His job was to report infractions of church law. We can thank the Puritans of American colonial society for an official called the nightwatch. His duty was to check on folks who went out at night. The Puritan authorities felt no one should leave his home at night without good reason. The nightwatch was to take into custody anyone with a story he didn't like. And the individual would appear in court the next morning for punishment unless he could come up with a better story for the judge. One suspects that in Puritan society a smile was sufficient to cause an arrest for suspicion of being joyful.

The ordinances directed that the nightwatch should "walk silently and slowly, now and then to stand still and listen in order to make discovery." How do you suppose they'd get along in Central Park today?

In addition to the nightwatch, the New England settlers gave us the tythingman. Unlike the constable or nightwatch who was charged with general supervision of the public, the tythingman was sort of an early version of today's neighborhood crime watch. The tythingman was to oversee ten of the neighboring families and to be on the lookout for crime, corruption, and sin. His specific duties were to discover any private unlicensed houses of entertainment, and the laws for the tythingmen directed them to catch Sabbath breakers and tipplers.

The tythingmen earned their keep with a percentage of the fines paid by offenders. But after a few years, even the New England Puritans were tired of these court appointed nosy neighbors, and even with payment of one half of the fines collected, recruitment of tythingmen became difficult. By the mid 1700s, the office of tythingman was left for the history books. Unfortunately, sin and corruption survived despite the early efforts of the constables, nightwatch, and tythingmen, and so, in the 1800s, the first police forces were organized in the Americas.

Of course, effective law enforcement depends mostly on the integrity of the official and the public acceptance of the law. The title of the official doesn't really matter. The great American jurist, Benjamin Cardozo, probably put it best when he said, "Officialdom, however it displays itself, is the husk, and what is precious is the person within."

Most of us think of Robin Hood as one of the good guys and the high sheriff of Nottingham as the bad guy. That's certainly the way television and the movies show it and who am I to argue with Hollywood. But the title sheriff is an old and honorable one and its history might be fun to know.

We all know the fellow chasing Robin Hood

was the high sheriff of Nottingham. He was called high sheriff because he was the chief sheriff rather than a deputy sheriff. Nottingham was not just Nottingham, but a political subdivision like our county. In Old England, the unit was called a shire—like Worcestershire Sauce—and each shire had a special representative of the king who was called a reeve. Every shire had a reeve—a shirereeve —later known as a sheriff and he served as a governor of the shire.

The job of sheriff was a top political post. He was the personal representative of the king, executed court orders, and collected royal rent and taxes. Prisoners were placed in the sheriff's care and he was also a judge in two courts of his own, one criminal and one civil. Every four to six weeks the sheriff convened the county courts.

The power of the early sheriff was awesome. He had what they called the bodyguard but what today we would call an army. The sheriff was, in fact, a military commander. Waging war prior to 1066 is usually credited to the king, but a check of the records will show more than one order being sent by the sheriff.

When William the Conqueror brought the Norman invasion to London's doorstep, he held his army in check to negotiate with the sheriff who was in charge of the city's defenses. Although the conqueror won the battle, the sheriff may have won the war, and William and his sons maintained the sheriff as one of the Crown's most prestigious posts.

Being named sheriff in Old England was both good news and bad news. There was no fixed salary, although many received handsome rewards for their loyal service to grateful kings. Others, however, ended their careers in debt and their land and possessions were seized by the new sheriff of the king. Some, like the high sheriff of Nottingham, became wealthy on the dark side of the law. Citizens were forced to pay tribute to the sheriff to avoid harassment from his bodyguards, or army. But this too had its risks and more than one sheriff ended his career in prison or a graveyard for his misdeeds.

The American image of a sheriff is a tall guy wearing a big white hat and boots with a couple of guns ready at hand. Quite a difference from the high sheriff's outfit, which was a velvet knee breeches suit. But they both wore a special badge.

Times have changed since the high sheriff of Nottingham chased Robin Hood and his band. But the post remains an important part of our legal system. Even today the sheriff has charge of jails and prisoners, and one of his most important jobs is serving the papers of the court and executing judgments and orders of the court.

One of the court officials of eighteenth-century France was called the rifleur. By definition, he was an official charged with supervision of the marketplace and enforcement of local police regulations. But in fact the rifleur was the most dreaded and detested public official in all France. Under cover of that simple title was the executioner of criminal sentences—privately called the headsman. The headsmen were the public executioners of France. They hanged for the king and guillotined for the republic.

Rifleurs and executioners

In 1789, there were about 160 headsmen in France. Their work was considered so detestable that they lived as outcasts and the executioner's commission passed from father to son—mostly because no one else wanted the job. They married the sons and daughters of other executioners and their only social life was in the company of other headsmen.

Until the time of the revolution, the post was a lucrative one. The rifleurs had the right of havage and could tax the market vendors. Most market vendors objected to paying the executioners tax, and when they did pay it would very carefully avoid the chalk mark on their arm which signaled that the executioner had been given his due.

The job of executioner was an odious one in the best of times, but during the terror of the French revolution it became particularly hideous. The courts of the new French republic dispatched thousands to the scaffolds where their heads parted company from their bodies. Executioners worked day and night and even rode circuit to cleanse the country of noble families and enemies of the republic.

Business was so good that ads appeared seeking additional "avengers of the people," as they were called, but the ads went unanswered. A few amateur executioners signed up and their brutality was so horrible that the work of the professional looked charitable.

The most famous name of the French executioners was Sanson. The first Sanson was appointed chief executioner of Paris in 1688, and the post remained in the Sanson family for nearly two hundred years. In 1778, Charles Henri Sanson was commissioned chief executioner of Paris by King Louis XVI, who fifteen years later had his head chopped off by the very executioner he had appointed.

During the terror Charles Henri Sanson almost single-handedly eliminated the French royal family. In addition to King Louis, Marie Antoinette rode in the Sanson tumbril—a little wooden cart used to take the condemned from the court to the scaffold—and then felt the blade of Sanson's guillotine.

The job was never an easy one and had its share of occupational hazards. Sanson's son was killed at work when he picked up one of the heads he had cut off to show the crowd. He slipped off the scaffold and was killed when he hit the ground.

But all good things come to an end—even for an executioner. By the mid 1800s business had fallen off. The job was no longer so lucrative and the Sanson holding the Paris post found himself heavily in debt. In 1847 he was jailed for his debts but made a deal with creditors and pawned the guillotine to get out of prison. Unfortunately an execution was scheduled before Sanson could get his killing machine out of pawn. The creditor refused to return the guillotine until he was paid. The government paid his bill, but poor old Sanson was sacked. He went into hiding and with him one of the most infamous names of the French revolution disappeared for all time.

The judge may be the "top banana" of the American courtroom, but the majordomo is someone called the bailiff. He's the "all rise" guy or gal who heralds the arrival of the judge and says the magic words that open the court for each new day's session. He calls and seats the jurors, swears in the witnesses, and keeps order in the courtroom.

For centuries the office of bailiff has been a key post in the legal community. But by comparison, today's bailiff is a mere shadow of his counterparts from yesteryear. In medieval times, the bailiff was the keeper of the royal fortress and personal representative of the lord of the manor. He managed the lord's estate, collected the rents, and disbursed the funds. While modern bailiffs play "second banana" to the judge, the bailiffs of Old England often were the judges. They had the power to arrest and hold accused criminals and to conduct jury inquests within their counties.

Historically, the title bailiff was synonymous with minister of the crown. The title was used to cover all those who had some official public authority and when the law imposed special duties on the sheriff or coroner or constable, they were counted as "bailiffs" of the king.

Today the bailiff is associated with the judge and the courts. But a few hundred years ago, the bailiff was the special agent of the sheriff and was the number one or two executive of county government.

In fact, the word *bailwick* was specifically coined to describe the office or territorial domain of the bailiff, and the high bailiffs of Old England even wore a colorful robe of office.

The English sheriff was normally the head of county government—appointed by and responsible only to the king. He collected taxes, served the king's writs, held accused criminals, ran the jail, and impaneled the juries. He was also a military leader and commanded the posse or army in each county.

But the job of sheriff was so awesome and complicated that he needed help and his chief assistant was found in the person of the bailiff. The bailiff operated in the subdivisions the way the sheriff operated in the county.

Neither the sheriff nor his bailiff received a salary, but lived the good life through their perks or benefits. They received commissions from the rents collected, fees from writs served, and the payments for prisoners in their custody. Then, too, as they traveled around the county, they could demand "hospitality" from local citizens.

As the years passed and the king's government became stronger and more central, the powers of the sheriffs and their bailiffs declined. Some bailiffs were a little too creative in finding fees. In many bailwicks, for example, a little "fee" paid to the bailiff could excuse a person from jury service. Eventually the local folks grew tired of these fee schemes and began to complain to the king. Sheriffs and bailiffs with money who commanded county armies were also a threat to the English kings. So, a more centralized legal system was developed which eliminated many of the bailiff's discretionary and fee raising powers.

Eventually, bailiffs became officers of the courts rather than executives in charge of district and county government. But the bailiffs hold a place of honor in the development of the common law and their authority even today is considerable.

So, the next time you need help at the local courthouse, check with the bailiff. You may well find that he or she is still the person really in charge.

If someone mentions Sing Sing, Alcatraz, the Bastille, or Devil's Island, our minds conjure up an image of men living in the dungeons and hell holes of the world's most infamous prisons. But of all the prisons of history, few summon an image more elegant or regal than the Tower of London.

Snuggled next to the Thames River this eerie

group of gray buildings is Europe's oldest palace, fortress, and prison. Its walls have housed England's arsenal, mint, treasury, crown jewels, and its courts of justice.

William the Conqueror began construction of the Tower shortly after the Battle of Hastings on the same site Julius Caesar had picked one thousand years earlier. Both great soldiers decided the location offered safety from attack by land on the one side and from attack by sea on the other.

The Tower was never a place for the common street thieves of London. It was a royal castle and a prison for the rich and powerful. Queens Anne Boleyn, Catherine Howard, and Jane Grey died on the Tower scaffold and three kings of the Scots, a French king, and several English kings found themselves locked in Tower chambers.

Ranulf Flambard has the distinction of being the first of the Tower's many prisoners and he was also the first to escape. Flambard was bishop of Durham and confidant to King William II. Using his position to squeeze money from noblemen, he soon became a hated figure, and when his protector died the new king quickly sent Flambard to the Tower. But after a few months of congenial confinement, he arranged a banquet for his captors where the wine flowed freely. When his guests were sufficiently drunk, the bishop slipped out and escaped into the pages of history. Sir Thomas Moore, the man for all seasons, died at the hands of an angry king within Tower walls as did the celebrated Sir Walter Raleigh. The

splendid robes of an archbishop of Canterbury could be sometimes seen in the prisoners' courtyard and Chief Justice Lord Jefferies was himself scheduled to feel the Tower executioner's ax. Judge Jefferies, however, escaped his fate by judiciously drinking himself to death.

The Tower, of course, is not just a tower, but a complex of towers. Within its walls you'll find the White Tower, the Bell Tower, the Cradle Tower, the Middle Tower, and among others one called Bloody Tower. Originally the Garden Tower, it was renamed Bloody Tower because of its many tragedies. The chief among these was the murder of the young princes Edward and Richard. The two boys disappeared in their sleep and it was nearly two hundred years later when their skeletons were found in a wooden chest in a staircase foundation.

Since the Tower is a fortress, a prison, and a royal palace, it is under the command of a special constable appointed by the king. But the Tower's most familiar sight is the yeoman of the guard in his scarlet and gold uniform topped off with the famous old beefeater hat. But as inmates would say, though the jailers be colorful, "it is no flattery to a prisoner to gild the jail."

Prisons rarely affect the course of history, but the Tower is an exception. The mystery, intrigue, and fate of Tower celebrities did, indeed, influence the destiny of England. Although Tower cells have long been empty, the man in the beefeater hat is still on hand to give you a tour and as the English nobility used to say, "It's a great place to visit, but you wouldn't want to live there."

We recognize Socrates as one of history's great philosophers; his teachings have been with us for nearly twenty-five hundred years. But one of his less profound observations was that children were more disobedient and defiant than when he was a child. Confucius made the same complaint several hundred years before Socrates. In fact, every older generation since the beginning of time has denounced the youngsters of the new generation.

A British newspaper in 1850 observed that juvenile delinquency was sweeping the country and reported that more than seventeen thousand children were housed in British jails.

London's most infamous prison, Newgate, was a school for crime, and the judges sent young and old to this British dungeon. The youngsters could then mingle with the worst of England's criminal element. A Newgate prisoner with ten or twenty convictions might have by his side a child of seven or eight.

In eighteenth century England 160 crimes carried the death penalty and judges didn't consider youth a mitigating factor. English courts record the execution of dozens of teenage offenders. A thirteen-year-old was hanged for taking a watch and a little girl of twelve died for stealing twenty cents from her

mistress. Government seemed to feel no special concern for society's young people.

Even in the United States government interest in how youngsters behave has been a recent development. Unless a youth committed a major crime his only contact with the state was with the cop on the beat. The first juvenile court didn't arrive on the scene until 1899. Its purpose was to protect the child from the harsh punishment of the adult criminal court.

But major efforts were eventually made by the American legal system to define the rights of children. At the turn of the century, legislators decided that young offenders should be removed from the adult criminal court system and placed in specialized juvenile courts. The aim was to rehabilitate rather than punish. But sentences varied and were often unfair and arbitrary, or even more severe than those given to adults. Furthermore, the early juvenile justice system deprived youngsters of most constitutional rights.

As a result, the Supreme Court outlined three precepts of juvenile rights. The first said that primary responsibility for raising children lies with parents. The second recognizes the state responsibility to intervene if the youngster is abused, neglected, or abandoned. The third says children are people and have individual rights.

The leading juvenile rights case is the 1967 decision of In Re Gault. The Supreme Court held juveniles were entitled to due process of law and had a right to notice of any charge filed against them, a right to counsel, a privilege against self incrimination, and a right to confront the complaining witnesses.

There are still some rights given to adults but denied to children. Juveniles have no right to a jury trial, no right to be indicted by a grand jury, no right to a public trial, and no right to bail.

The lot of the juvenile is still less than perfect and adults will always view youngsters as delinquents. But if you're familiar with the life and times of Oliver Twist or any other of old Europe's young ragamuffin street thieves, you'll have to agree that today's juvenile courts offer a much better system.

The hands of history's assassins have washed in the blood of emperors, czars, kaisers, and kings. Carlos the Jackal, one of the twentieth century's premier terrorist/assassins, said violence is the one language Western democracies can understand. But history's legacy of violence has not been limited to the West; it has touched the four corners of our round world.

Presidents and prime ministers of recent time stand side by side with the noble princes of nations past as victims of the assassin. Indira Gandhi has joined the Mahatma—that legendary Gandhi of India's history who was also felled by the assassin's bullet. Anwar Sadat, John Kennedy, Julius Caesar, Aldo Moro, Abraham Lincoln, Richard II, Pak Choong He are but a few of the names from the long list of leaders taken by the assassin's hand.

The word *assassin* comes from a secret Moslem religious order whose fanatic members terrorized and killed the Christian crusaders. The legal system is frustrated by the assassin since the law acts after the fact, and, historically, the successful assassin often became the new caesar or king.

But the American assassin has more often been from the lunatic fringe than from any organized terror or religious group. The first would-be assassin of an American president was Richard Lawrence who tried to kill Andrew Jackson in 1835. Since that attempt on Jackson's life, ten other presidents have been targets of the assassin. Lincoln, Garfield, McKinley, both Roosevelts, Truman, Kennedy, Nixon, Ford, and Reagan were all prey of the American assassin.

Of the thirteen killers or would-be killers of American presidents, nine actually went to trial. The insanity plea was used in America's first assassination trial as well as the last. Both ended in acquittal. Jackson's would-be assassin died in a mental institution, but we can only speculate on John Hinckley's future.

The insanity defense was used for most of these potential assassins. All of the defendants were mentally unstable, but the insanity plea was not always accepted. McKinley's assassin, Leon Czolgosz, was convicted in a short, eight-hour trial. Although generally acknowledged as insane, he was nevertheless electrocuted. Giuseppe Zangara attempted to kill FDR but missed and killed Chicago's Mayor Cermak. The man was convicted of the mayor's murder and sentenced to death. Garfield's assassin, Charles J. Guiteau, had a seventy-two-day trial, during which he attempted to prove his insanity. The jury rejected the plea and ordered him hanged. Insanity pleas for the two women who attempted to assassinate President Ford were rejected and both are serving life sentences in prison.

John Schrank was tried for his attempt to kill Teddy Roosevelt. He was declared insane and sent to a hospital. While on the way to the mental institution Schrank was asked by a guard if he liked to hunt. "Only bull moose," the assassin answered.

The turmoil caused by the assassin is often enormous. The death of a leader can signal the beginning of national riots. Sometimes even wars are blamed on the assassination of a political leader. Fortunately, the United States government has been stable enough to survive the assassin's terror and to make an orderly transition of leadership from one president to another. We might remember the words of the Irish leader who said, "It is not those who can inflict the most, but those who can suffer the most who will conquer."

The Eighth Amendment to the United States Constitution protects us from cruel and un-usual punishment. The problem, of course, is to decide just what those terms mean. Civil libertarians argue the death penalty is cruel and unusual, and an annual parade of death sentence cases makes its way to the United States Supreme Court.

Life sentences for multiple offenders might be considered cruel and unusual, and those Texas sentences of from five hundred to one thousand years in the penitentiary are at least a little strange. The Star Chamber Court of Old England used to split noses and cut off ears as punishment. The French made liberal use of the guillotine while the Romans eliminated undesirables with crucifixion. Middle eastern countries chop off the hand of a thief and stone the adulteress. And let's not forget body stretching by rope or rack and the infamous iron maiden, a hollow iron statue shaped like a woman and lined with iron spikes to impale the enclosed victim.

No look at crime and punishment would be complete, however, without an examination of the five punishments of imperial China. For nearly five thousand years the Chinese legal system relied on the Wu Hsing or the five corporal punishments. The original five punishments were tatooing, amputation of the nose, amputation of one foot, castration, and death.

When the T'ang Code was adopted by the Chinese emperor in 653, it incorporated the five punishments but changed them slightly to include beating with a light stick, then a heavy stick, penal servitude, lifetime exile, and violent death. Within each category there were varying degrees of punishment.

The number of blows with a heavy or light stick changed according to the severity of the crime. The years of penal servitude varied, and the distance one could be sent in exile stretched.

Death sentences were divided into death by strangulation and by decapitation. Strangulation was considered more humane because the spirit could return to a whole body. For treason or murdering a parent, the penalty of old China was death by slicing—or the lingering death. The offender was tied to a cross and then with a series of painful, but not mortal cuts the body was sliced beyond recognition. As terrible as it sounds, the punishment was not intended as a torture but rather to destroy the future as well as the present life of the offender. It reflected the feeling that the defendant was unworthy to exist either in body or spirit. A spirit could only appear by assuming the dead person's body, and small pieces weren't enough to hold the spirit.

During the period of the T'ang Code, there were 233 capital offenses—144 by strangulation and 89 by decapitation. As the years passed the codes changed and new offenses were added. Under the Ch'ing dynasty from 1644 to 1911, the code contained a grand total of 3,987 punishable offenses.

But the Oriental or Middle Eastern peoples were not the only ones to excel at cruel and unusual punishment. The particularly obnoxious offender in Old England was first half hanged—making sure he was not dead. Then his private parts were cut off, also not killing him. Then he was disemboweled and finally his body was quartered. Now that, my friends, is cruel and unusual punishment and explains in part why our forefathers gave us the Eighth Amendment.

Every once in a while when I was a kid a little chocolate would melt in my shirt or pants pocket. That was before M&M's and it always earned me a good scolding. When my kids dropped bubble gum in my shoe or spilled their milk in the car, they got a good scolding and being scolded is part of the growing up process.

But there's a big difference between being scolded and being a scold. At common law, a scold was a troublemaker who spent the day gossiping, spreading rumors, brawling, and being an all around pain in the public peace.

The common scold was a tongue wagger and when that tongue wagged too often, it was time to call the law. In the Middle Ages the Church and the State operated hand in glove, and the law punished both crime and sin. Of the seven mortal sins, three were of the tongue—idolotry, blasphemy, and false witness—and the scold represented a serious religious and legal problem.

Throughout Europe, and particularly in England, the usual punishment for a scold was a few ups and downs in the ducking stool. That was a chair put on the end of a little swinging crane. The scold was strapped to the chair, swung out over the water, and then dropped three or four times. That gave the appearance of diving into the water like a duck.

Sermons were preached on the evils of being a scold and the leading preachers published books with such titles as *The Taming of the Tongue, The Poisons of the Tongue,* and one called *The Direction for the Government of the Tongue According to God's Word.*

Of course, the poets and songwriters of the times got into the act. One wrote "Keep a good tongue in your head, for here's a good woman in every respect but only her tongue breeds all the defect."

Another wrote, "I do not disparage—to hinder their marriage—but wish both old and young—great heed to take—when the choice they make—for virtue's sake—no venomous snake—stings like a woman's tongue." A popular proverb of the times outlined three damned things in a house: a leaking roof, a smoking chimney, and a railing wife.

Most of the persons accused of being scolds were women and the ducking stool was reserved almost exclusively for them. The law felt that ducking the local gossip would improve her manners. Of course, it also drowned a few.

Bringing one of the local ladies to justice and the ducking stool was a festive occasion for the local community. It usually took place on market day; the accused wore a necklace of wooden tongues around her neck and carried a bundle of straw as a symbol of contempt. Chapter three of the Epistle of St. James says that the tongue is a fire. What better to put out a fire than water?

Sharp tongues are no longer punished by criminal courts, but civil actions of libel and slander still exist. So the warning of Ecclesiasticus, "The stroke of the tongue breaketh the bones, many have fallen by the edge of the sword, but not so many as have fallen by the tongue," still rings true and, as Washington Irving said, "A sharp tongue is still the only edge tool that grows keener with constant use."

Special Occasions

While Cromwell and his armies were busy stomping out heathens in the countryside, the Puritans in Parliament were busy stomping out Christmas.

When it comes to world-class celebrations of the Christmas season the legal profession certainly takes first place honors. The mirth and merriment of the annual holiday has touched all. Even the periwigged, black-robed judges and barristers of Old England fell prey to the high spirits of Christmas.

Christmas was such an important time in England that each great household appointed a special person to plan and direct the festivities. They were given the title Lord of Misrule or Abbot of Unreason, and they reigned complete with a crest of holly and the motto "semper feriano" or "always keeping the holiday." Their function was to organize the games and keep up a continuous round of merriment from Christmas Eve to the Twelfth Night ceremony.

One would hardly expect to find the beginnings of these great pageants of Christmas in the grave and dusty retreats of law. Yet, it was with the four Inns of Court that we find the start of these mighty celebrations. The Inns of Court are the legal training grounds for the judges and barristers of the British legal system.

During the sixteenth and seventeenth centuries, the Inns of Court made Christmas part of the adversary system. They began to compete with each other to see which could set up the most splendid pageant. The ceremony of mirth and merriment continued on each of the twelve nights of Christmas beginning with an evening feast. After the gala dinner, sports, games, and dancing continued through the night until breakfast.

In 1640, the Lord of Misrule rode through the City of Norwich, dressed in silk and tinsel, preceded by twelve persons dressed to depict each month of the year—perhaps a forerunner of our Thanksgiving or Rose Bowl parades.

Of course, as frequently happens, the merriment sometimes got out of hand. Each year, the Christmas pageants became more extravagant, involving more money, more elaborate costumes, bigger parades, but less humor and with more people offended. The situation became so outrageous and costly that at one time the Scottish parliament passed a statute making the appointment of a Lord of Misrule or Abbot of Unreason a crime. An English judge once sentenced a cobbler to be hanged for acting the part of Robin Hood in a Christmas play. Fortunately,

the local citizens rioted and forcibly rescued the cobbler from that undeserved fate.

The society of Gray's Inn found themselves in trouble in 1527. Their pageant was a political satire disguised as Christmas revelry. Unfortunately, the disguise was a little thin and the lawyers and judges offended a cardinal of the Church. To teach the gentlemen of Gray's Inn that they were responsible for all wounds caused, even accidental, the cardinal let the ingenius authors celebrate the final days of Christmas in jail.

For a number of reasons—most of them good—The Lord of Misrule and the Abbot of Unreason now celebrate Christmas only in the pages of history. But many of the Christmas traditions we enjoy today—the pageants, parades, songs, and games—were developed by those usually somber folks in black robes and powdered wigs.

One of the inevitable arrivals of the holiday season is the traditional gift calendar. Whether it's the desktop model from the local insurance agency or the wall hanging variety from the florist, it's just a matter of time before one arrives in your mailbox. The holiday displays at bookstores and card shops offer dozens of calendars to choose from. There's the Currier and Ives design with its quiet, understated elegance; the exercise calendars of Jane Fonda or Richard Simmons; the animal calendars featuring dogs, cats, horses, or, if you prefer, even bunnies. And, if you're in the right bookstore and you look hard enough, you may even discover something called the Newgate calendar.

This one is really different from any that I've mentioned and if you have a friend who's interested in crime and punishment, the Newgate calendar would make a superior gift. Among the many differences from other calendars, this one goes backward and chronicles the lives and times of some of the more interesting inmates who were sentenced to Newgate prison. The Newgate Calendar and Criminal Recorder is really the four-volume work of two attorneys named Andrew Knapp and William Baldwin. It's not exactly hot off the press, having been first published in 1824, but considering that the history of Newgate prison dates back to the eleventh century, it's a relatively recent publication.

The coversheet of each volume announces that the Newgate calendar comprised certain memoirs of the more notorious characters convicted of outrages on the laws of England. According to the attorney authors, it contains "anecdotes, observations, speeches, confessions, and the last exclamations of sufferers." While Messrs. Knapp and Baldwin may have been learned in the law, the sermons they offer at the close of each inmate biography would do a preacher proud.

The characters of the Newgate calendar include a chap known as the flying highwayman, a rogue commonly referred to as Sixteen-String Jack, and another who was dubbed Half-Hanged Smith. Half-Hanged Smith dangled for nearly fifteen minutes before a reprieve arrived at the prison. He was cut down and revived and was then able to tell the wide-eyed spectators of the strange half-in, half-out feeling experienced during his short stretch.

The flying highwayman earned his name when his horse was seen jumping bridges and barriers during the course of his many escapes, and Sixteen-String Jack was so named because he wore breeches with eight strings at each knee. These colorful characters shared the same rope as a final reward for their misdeeds.

But of all the villains chronicled in the Newgate calendar, the legendary buccaneer, Captain William Kidd, is perhaps the most interesting. The very mention of his name conjures up visions of the bearded pirate wearing gold earrings, drinking his rum, counting his doubloons and pieces of eight, and lounging around romantic island paradises. At his last port of call, Execution Dock, in 1701 Captain Kidd was hanged for murder and piracy. Even then, he was providentially given a few extra moments to repent when his body weight broke the hangman's rope and he was hauled back to the dock for a second more successful try.

Anyone interested in the history of crime and the punishments of law will find the pages of the Newgate calendar fascinating reading. All the characters chronicled are worthy of nomination to a criminal hall of fame. Exciting people to have known or to read about, but certainly not, if you'll forgive the pun, the sort of folks you'd want to hang around with.

Ever since the Pilgrims invited the Indians to dinner, the turkey has held a place of honor on the Thanksgiving tables of America. Benjamin Franklin was so impressed with the turkey that he once suggested it replace the bald eagle as the national bird. The eagle, said Franklin, was a bird of bad moral character. It was lazy, sneaky, and lived off the work of others. The turkey, on the other hand, was a bird of courage and would not hesitate to attack any British grenadier who invaded its farmyard.

Of course, the majesty of the bald eagle won out. The turkey may taste good, but it doesn't look good. In fact, it looks so silly that over the years the word *turkey* has come to mean things other than just dinner. A movie that's a box office failure is called a turkey and more than one sporting event has been lost because of some turkey on the playing field.

Now when it comes to that second kind of turkey, the law struts right along with the best of them. In the category of silly and stupid laws, nominations for gobbler awards include the Illinois law banning the sale of ice cream sodas on the Sabbath, which caused an Evanston drugstore owner to come up with a new concoction which he called the "sundae." Also in the running is the New Jersey ordinance that prohibited people from slurping their soup, the Ohio ordinance outlawing ownership of bathtubs, the West Vir-

ginia law prohibiting the clergy from joke telling on Sunday, the New York ordinance that outlawed horses from sleeping in Brooklyn apartment bathtubs, and the Nebraska law that made it possible to arrest the parents of any child that burped in church.

In the category of laws destined to fail, anything aimed at the regulation of booze, gambling, or prostitution is eligible for a gobbler award; prohibition has to be one of history's great turkey laws. That noble experiment organized crime and institutionalized corruption. Although designed to eliminate the evils of whiskey drinking, prohibition lasted only thirteen years and left America with 23 percent more illegal speakeasies than there had been legal taverns before the law was passed. Gambling laws have been so spectacularly unsuccessful that many state governments are now in the gambling business and if you think prostitution is gone, just check with a hotel's concierge.

Nominations in the final gobbler award category for inept laws include the Pennsylvania statute that says you can't shoot a gun during or after a wedding ceremony and thereby removing the dangers in shotgun weddings; the Idaho law which left some husbands out in the cold by making it illegal to sleep in dog houses; and the Ohio law that made it legal for a wife to destroy her husband's hunting and fishing "junk."

No doubt other great turkey laws lurk about the provinces, but at least be thankful that most of the laws nominated for these gobbler awards have long since disappeared.

Some years ago in France, on the first day of April, a young lady appeared in a criminal court charged with stealing a friend's watch. She denied the charge and the judge sent a messenger to search her apartment. When the messenger returned with the stolen watch, the quick thinking thief shouted, "April Fools." "Very good," said the judge, "so good you may spend until April 1 next year in jail preparing another."

The tradition of playing legitimate pranks on April 1 has been around for centuries and comes to us from our European ancestors. The April fool in Scotland is called a cuckoo, in France an April fish, and in England they're called April gobs or April noddies.

The most popular form of April fooling is the fool's errand—sending someone to buy some pigeon's milk, for example, or to the library for a copy of the history of Adam's grandfather.

April Fools' Day, never a legal holiday, has been called a holiday of the mind, not of the state. New Year's Day, on the other hand, was and is a legal holiday in most nations. Throughout the Middle Ages, New Year's Day came on the twenty-fifth of March. But that day often fell during Holy Week and sometimes even on Good Friday. So the celebration of the New Year was postponed until April 1, with one of the traditions being the giving of gifts.

In the sixteenth century, the reformed Gregorian calendar was adopted and that called for the New Year to begin on January 1. It took time for some folks to get used to the change, and jokesters would pay New Year's visits to friends on April 1. They would bring mock or joke gifts in an effort to make April fools of their forgetful hosts. Eventually even the slowest person knew the calendar had changed, but the practical jokes lived on.

So on the first of April be careful out there. If you have to return a call from Mr. Bear, make sure you're not calling the city zoo; you might also check your coattails for a "kick me" sign. In the spirit of the fool's day you might want to wish your friends a Happy New Year. They might think you're joking, but we'll know better—you're just a few centuries behind!

The parliamentarians of Old England would have been tickled to death with the Dr. Seuss story *How the Grinch Stole Christmas*. After all, a few hundred years earlier they tried to do the same thing themselves. The parliamentarians were Puritans, and they controlled England's governing body during the time of Cromwell's rebellion against King Charles I. The Puritans operated on the theory that if it hurt, it was good for you and if it was fun, it was a sin. The idea of Christmas being celebrated with lights and laughter and food and drink was more than the somber Puritans could stomach. So while Cromwell and his armies were busy stomping out heathens in the countryside, the Puritans in Parliament were busy stomping out Christmas.

They began chipping away at Christmas celebrations in 1642 by passing ordinances outlawing the performance of the traditional holiday plays. The next year they ordered the marketplaces to remain open for business on Christmas while churches were warned not to decorate for the holiday and to be closed on Christmas Day.

In 1644, Christmas fell on the last Wednesday of December. The Puritans had designated the last Wednesday of each month as a time for fast and humiliation. To avoid any confusion as to how Christmas was to be observed, Parliament passed something called "An Ordinance for the Better Observance of the Feast of the Nativity of Christ." Citizens were ordered to fast on Christmas and to remember the sins of their forefathers who had wrongfully turned Christmas into a festive and happy occasion. A Puritan preacher applauded the new ordinance saying, "God by a providence, hath buried this Feast in a Fast," and he prayed it would remain that way forever.

Parliament set an example by holding a session on Christmas Day, and the citizens of England were given one of the gloomiest yuletide seasons in history. Yet the people persisted in celebrating Christmas until finally, in 1647, Parliament passed an act abolishing Christmas altogether.

Of course, the Commonwealth under Cromwell and his Puritan followers didn't last forever, and when it ended the town criers heralded the news, "Cromwell is dead; long live Christmas!" When King Charles II took the throne in 1660, the yuletide festivities were finally restored to the English people. But in the colonies, the king's subjects were still fighting for the right to celebrate their holiday season. The Massachusetts legislature, or general court as it was called, had passed an act making it a criminal offense to celebrate any religious holiday, especially Christmas. The act imposed a five shilling fine on any who violated the law; other colonial assemblies passed similar statutes. In 1722 when the governor of Massachusetts suggested that the legislature adjourn over Christmas, the Puritan members of the assembly created an uproar and pointed out that failure to work on Christmas would violate the legislature's law. The governor's suggestion was nevertheless accepted, and when the members went home to spend the Christmas holiday with family and friends the criminal act was quietly laid to rest.

Fortunately those days are gone and, we can hope, forever. Today we celebrate our religious holidays however we choose, and our holiday gift from history is the reminder that even good, well-meaning people can make bad decisions under the influence of religious zeal.

Tools of the Law

The Domesday Book represents the greatest administrative achievement of any medieval kingship.

Most of us agree with the idea that a person is innocent until proven guilty. After all, that's the American way. This is a democracy, a free country. We don't live in Nazi Germany or Communist Russia. But sometimes that ideal bumps heads with the practical realities of life, and nowhere is the collision seen better than in the bail bond program.

The accused may be innocent until proven guilty, but a voice inside often says, "He wouldn't be here if he hadn't done something." The dilemma is this. If the individual is innocent until proven guilty, he shouldn't be punished before his day in court. But if he's guilty and we don't hold him he may run. So, enter the bail bond; it offers a defendant freedom until trial, and forfeits money if he fails to appear.

The word *bail* comes from a Norman French word describing a bucket or scoop used to dip water out of a boat. In today's street language, bail means getting out of jail. Just as you bail water out of a boat, you now bail a person out of prison.

Historically, bail came from an old English program called hostageship. A person was literally held hostage until the promise of another was fulfilled. The bail system also borrows from the English laws used to process debts. Under a concept called wergeld, someone who was accused of a civil wrong posted money to reimburse that wrong in the event he was later found at fault.

When someone was accused of a crime, it was the sheriff's job to hold the person. But the prisons were terrible and expensive, and the traveling judges of Old England might not be back for months. Understandably, the sheriff was happy to rid himself of this job, and if a landholder would vouch for a defendant, the sheriff would turn over the accused. This was referred to as private jailing or as the Duke's living prison. The sureties who vouched for the defendant then became his private jailers.

Before King Henry II, criminal cases were brought by private citizens. An individual would accuse someone under oath and would then post bond to cover damages if the charges proved false. The accused was treated as probably guilty and imprisoned until trial. But Henry II put the crown in charge of criminal justice. A grand jury was formed, but just a suspicion or rumor was enough to bring a criminal charge. With proceedings started by rumor or hearsay, there was a greater possibility that the accused was not guilty. The bail release program became more important and so began the slow evolution of today's bail bond system. The English Bill of Rights of 1689 guarded against excessive bail as does the Eighth Amendment to our Constitution.

The purpose of bail, simply put, is to ensure that the accused will appear for trial. Making that system work, however, is not so simple. We have all heard horror stories of defendants who robbed or raped while out on bail. But there are others who have been victims of the bail system—the poor, the young, the vocal advocates of unpopular causes, those who have languished in prison for months before unjust charges were dismissed by trial.

In recent years, serious efforts have been made to reform the bail system and more reforms are still needed. But as we seek to improve the program, let's not forget the principle involved—the spirit of the bail bond system is to establish a procedure whereby the accused may stay out of jail until a trial has found him guilty. Or, better put, it supports the idea that a person is presumed innocent until proven guilty.

Every now and then I hear a lawyer tell the story of the new attorney who rushed back to the law firm after his first trial and announced, "Justice triumphed." The senior partner looked up and immediately said, "Appeal." Some people think that story is funny—some don't. But no one ever questions the right of an individual to appeal a judgment.

Yet, the process of appeal we enjoy today was not always so commonplace. The American legal system is a combination of the legal practices of several European countries. Although we rely mainly on the British common law, our English cousins adopted Roman and Germanic principles long before the *Mayflower* sailed to the American colonies.

In France, an appeal was a direct attack on the court rendering the judgment. It was a dishonor and a failure of duty to participate in a false judgment. Anyone involved was subject to attack—witnesses and judges alike. If the judgment was proved to be false, the judges and witnesses were punished but the judgment remained.

The French medieval legal scholars said that the false judgment appeal should lead to penalties and damages against the false judges and not to a reversal because the party who won the judgment should not lose his claim to the fault of another. The appeal was settled by a duel between all the judges and aggrieved parties. The appellant usually didn't want to fight them all, so the chief judge would appoint one to do battle on behalf of his colleagues.

The Romans developed a different appeal system which led to a correction of the judgment rather than a punishment of the judges. Understandably, French judges urged the adoption of the Roman system, and King Louis IX abolished the judicial duel in favor of the Roman appeal system. That not only improved the appeal process but had the additional effect of improving trial practice. Witnesses, always reluctant to get involved, became more willing to testify when the potential of a later duel was removed.

British judges were apparently better organized with a more effective lobby. They eliminated the appellate judicial duel centuries earlier than the French. The last important judicial duel in England—unique because it was between a man and a dog—took place in 1400 and was really a trial by combat rather than an appeal. One of the local barons had been murdered by his friend. The only witness to the murder was the baron's faithful greyhound. The dog howled and kept watch over the burial spot until he finally attracted the attention of the servants. They dug up the spot where the dog had been scratching and found the body. Later, every time the baron's killer visited the estate, the usually docile dog would attack him. When the king heard of these strange events, he ordered a trial by combat between the dog and the suspect. At the start of the battle the dog attacked his master's murderer with a frenzy. He quickly grabbed the killer by the throat and wrestled him to the ground. In order to survive, the man confessed his crime. A few days later, he was swinging at the end of the king's rope and the nobleman's remains were given a proper burial.

The dog, of course, was never able to speak. But if he had, one would expect that he, too, would have announced, "Justice triumphed."

In the mid 1600s two British physicians named Meade and Woodward had a professional disagreement and decided to settle the matter with a duel. One hopes that they were better doctors than they were swordsmen, for in the process of dueling, Woodward slipped and fell to the ground. "Take your life," said the magnanimous Dr. Meade. Woodward, lying prostrate, looked up and replied acidly, "Anything but your physique."

That duel was remembered for its humor, but most such combats were anything but funny. The word *duel* comes from a combination of the Latin words *bellum* and *duo*, meaning "war" and "two." Today if someone insults your family or accuses you of some evil act, you use the courts to sue for slander or defamation. But a few hundred years ago, no one worth his salt would think of accepting a court judgment or money for a grievous insult. Those chivalrous folks of yesteryear demanded satisfaction on the fighting fields with a duel of honor.

Actually, as bad as it was, the duel was a step in the direction of humanity and law. It replaced the murderous assaults of the fifteenth century known as killing affrays. A group of assassins were hired to stalk the enemy and kill by ambush. So the prospect of a fair fight between two men armed with equal weapons made dueling a respectable legal remedy.

Naturally, there were laws governing the duel. The accepted Code Duello became known as the Twenty-six Commandments. It outlined who must apologize first, which insults were greater, what to do if swords were used, and how many pistol shots might be fired. Commandment twelve covered firing in the air. Since the challenger ought not to have challenged without first being offended, firing in the air was dishonorable and not permitted.

In the not very happy history of the duel, we find them being fought in strange circumstances—in locked rooms, in water, and some even in the dark. Emerson gives us a tongue-in-cheek tale of a London duel between an Englishman and a Frenchman. The seconds put out the lights and left the room. The Englishman, not wanting to hurt his rival, fired up the chimney, hitting the Frenchman.

The practice of dueling was also a regular remedy for offended Americans until the late 1800s. The list of American celebrities who sought satisfaction on the fields of honor include Andrew Jackson, Henry Clay, Aaron Burr, John Hancock, Sam Houston, James Bowie, and Winfield Scott. Even Abe Lincoln accepted a challenge at one point in his career, but in keeping with his reputation for wisdom, Honest Abe failed to appear at the appointed time and place. Fortunately, as the years of the nineteenth century passed, public confidence in the legal system grew and the duel of honor fell into public disfavor. State after state passed legislation making the duel illegal, but well into the twentieth century the oath of office for many public officials included a pledge not to fight the duel.

The absurdity of the whole process is probably best put by a celebrated French duelist. He had told an officer of the guard that he smelled like a goat and the man drew his sword to avenge the insult. "Put up your sword you fool," said the duelist. "If you kill me, you'll not smell any better, and if I kill you, you'll smell a damned sight worse." Unfortunately, it took society a long time to accept the simple logic of this remark, but finally the lesson was learned.

The reliability of public records is taken for granted in today's society. We expect birth certificates, marriage licenses, deeds, and mortgages to reflect accurate information. After all, they are official records and we rely upon them. But it wasn't always so and the foundation of today's public record system comes from a work we call the Domesday Book.

The Domesday Book was the product of a great survey ordered by William the Conqueror. When he was crowned king on Christmas Day in 1066, all of England's land became his. Those who had backed the Norman invasion of England expected to make a profit, so the king needed to raise revenue for the government. But before the conqueror could divide the spoils or set taxes, he needed to know what was available.

So, in 1085, the king sent representatives into every shire or county with orders to find out who owned what and where. That inquiry or inquest was called a "descripto," which means both to write down and to describe. During the inquest, residents described the land where they lived and in whose name it was held. They also catalogued the number of acres and counted the horses, cows, chickens, fisheries, and any other item that the king could use to collect taxes on or reward his friends with.

The Domesday Book was our first public record and the beginning of modern English history. Before that time a record was simply held in the memory of a responsible citizen, so the Domesday Book represents the greatest administrative achievement of any medieval kingship.

No one is actually quite certain why it's called the Domesday Book. The book simply calls itself a "descripto." One story says it's because the book was first housed in a Chapel of Winchester or in Domus Dei, the House of God. Another story tells us that *Domes* means judgment and that the judgments of local courts had much to do with the book's production.

Probably the best explanation comes from Richard Fitznigel, the treasurer of England, who wrote in 1179, "This book is called by the natives Domesday—that is, the day of judgment. For as the sentence of that strict and terrible last account cannot be evaded, so when this book is appealed to . . . , its sentence cannot be set aside." The local citizens compared the work of the great inquest to the book by which one day we will all be judged.

Our modern bureaucracy may also have been born with the Domesday Book. The work of that great inquest, done in the eleventh century, was ordered in triplicate. Testimony was taken in the towns and villages of the realm from English and Norman witnesses. These witnesses were called jurors because they took an oath (*jurer*) before they testified. Nearly two dozen major questions were asked of each juror—not once, not twice, but three times. The land was to be described as it was in the time of King Edward, as it was when William gave it, and finally as it was at the present time. Summaries were sent to the king at Winchester, and local scribes compiled the information to produce the Domesday Book. Somewhere in the heavens today, those scribes look at our computers and word processors and ask, "Where were you when we needed you?"

Tucked away in the file cabinets of the law, somewhere past the ipso's and the facto's, there's a folder marked The Great Writ. A writ is nothing more than an order from a court to do or not to do a certain thing. For example, courts issue writs of assistance and execution, entry and error, ejection and possession, restitution and review. But over the long and bumpy road traveled by the developers of our democracy, the writ of habeas corpus—called by Sir William Blackstone the great writ of liberty—became something special both for the people and for the law.

The writ of habeas corpus was the process by which the prisoners of evil kings and unjust bishops were freed. Early courts and judges were agents of the king. The judicial system wasn't independent nor did it protect the citizens. Instead, it was a tool of the establishment used by wealthy landlords and the church to enforce orders. The writ of habeas corpus could expose the deep secrets of the prison keepers and make public the reasons for a citizen's confinement.

An old maxim of the law tells us that "justice delayed is justice denied," and in Old England it was sometimes delayed for years. People were jailed without bond to await trial for real or imagined wrongs against the ruling class. Then after the long wait, they were often convicted and jailed for little more than having bad manners. But the great writ gave the champions of personal liberty a weapon to use in their battle to win freedom for the people. When a citizen was jailed for insulting the king or for challenging the pope's authority, it was habeas corpus that came to the rescue. Literally translated habeas corpus means "you should have the body." The writ commands a prison chief to bring forth his prisoner so that the reasons for imprisonment can be examined by the court.

In the aftermath of the trial of William Penn, the writ first gained prominence as a weapon for freedom fighters. Penn was a Quaker and vocal critic of the religious policies of King Charles. The king had Penn arrested and directed the jury to convict him, but the jury, led by one Mr. Bushell, found Penn not guilty. The king was outraged and fined the jury. When Bushell refused to pay he was marched off to prison, but a writ of habeas corpus focused attention on Bushell's illegal imprisonment and he was set free. The writ of habeas corpus was thus placed as a keystone in the development of human rights.

The founders of the new American republic understood the value of the great writ and protected the concept in the First Article of the Constitution. A classic American definition for habeas corpus came from an Illinois judge when he freed James Montgomery, a black man convicted of rape. Montgomery had served twenty-six years of a life sentence and habeas corpus was his last chance. During the review the judge found that the prosecution suppressed evidence showing the victim was a feeble-minded woman who died in an institution prior to trial and had died still a virgin. In his opinion the judge said, "This great Writ has been a sword and shield in a long struggle for freedom. . . . It is a potent weapon against tyranny in every form and brings to book those who . . . scorn . . . human rights."

So the file folder marked The Great Writ figures prominently in the file cabinet of American legal practice as containing a guardian of our inalienable rights to Life, Liberty, and the pursuit of Happiness.

In modern times, amnesties have become a routine part of most peace treaties. Although the treaties ending the Second World War contained no general amnesty clauses, Norway, the Netherlands, Japan, Germany, Belgium, and France passed separate amnesty acts for their citizens. Historically, most amnesties have been honored by the involved governments, although the Russians gave amnesty a black mark when their government executed several sailors involved in the 1905 Sailors' Revolt even though amnesty had been promised.

America's first involvement with amnesty began in the Whiskey Rebellion of 1794. When the farmers of western Pennsylvania refused to pay the new whiskey tax, President Washington sent in an army larger than the one he had commanded during the war with England. The army quickly got the attention of the farmers and the rebellion collapsed. Washington then set the precedent for reconciliation and issued a proclamation of amnesty for the rebel farmers. U.S. presidents have since issued ten amnesty proclamations and the Congress has also been involved in acts of amnesty and pardon.

President Andrew Johnson's Christmas amnesty of 1868 was a major American amnesty proclamation. It gave a universal and unconditional amnesty for all involved in the Civil War, including a full pardon for Civil War political activities. The legal memory of the war was officially erased by the amnesty.

Twentieth-century American amnesty efforts have not faired well. Eugene Debbs, the socialist party leader imprisoned for antiwar activities was pardoned on Christmas Day in 1921 by Warren Harding. Amnesty requests for Debbs and about one thousand other political activists were unsuccessful. Many of the World War I activists stayed in jail until pardoned by Coolidge in 1924—six years after the war—and a general amnesty was never declared.

One of the stumbling blocks to the passage of the Simpson-Mazzoli Immigration bill was the so-called amnesty provision. It made aliens in the country since 1977 eligible for permanent resident status even if they were here illegally. The government would forget how they got here and that forgetfulness is why it was an amnesty.

The meaning of amnesty is "forgetfulness." It comes from the Greek word *amnestia*, which means to erase the memory of past events. Governments have used amnesty to erase the legal memory of certain crimes, usually political. Amnesty is the forgetfulness of the offense as opposed to pardon, which is the forgiveness of the offense.

One of the earliest recorded amnesties was the Greek amnesty of 403 B.C. A group of wealthy military leaders took control of the government of Athens. They didn't care much for criticism, so the more vocal opponents of their government disappeared. As a result, hundreds of the good citizens of Athens took to the hills. Aristotle tells us of the civil war they started which eventually brought the Board of Ten, or governing body of Athens, to its knees. The board then restored democracy and welcomed the citizens back to Athens under a general amnesty declaration.

The United States has never declared a general amnesty for draft dodgers or deserters, and amnesty requests for Vietnam protestors caused a heated national debate but were not successful.

But overall, amnesty has played an important part in restoring peace to divided societies. Although the illegal aliens covered by the Simpson-Mazzoli bill haven't caused civil war, they have created a tough political problem which the Congress is attempting to solve through an old and honorable remedy called amnesty.

Personalities of the Law

Benedict Arnold was probably the greatest fighting general in the service of the Continental army, but he lives in history as America's best known traitor.

When John Wilkes Booth assassinated Abraham Lincoln, he dishonored the name of a great champion of personal liberty. The earlier John Wilkes was a seventeenth-century English politician who became a hero of the American Revolution. He supported the colonial call for independence, and his personal battle with King George III changed the arrest law of England and formed the foundation for our Bill of Rights. But Wilkes was also a colorful old rogue whose sharp tongue and pen kept him in constant trouble. He once remarked that he "loved his king so much he hoped never to see another," a statement in keeping with his motto, "Be as impudent as you can!"

While serving in the British Parliament, Wilkes anonymously published a wicked little pamphlet called *North Briton*. It called the king an imbecile and ridiculed the government so often that the king set out to get rid of both the paper and its editor. When *North Briton* No. 45 accused George of national betrayal, the king could stand it no more and called for a general arrest warrant.

A general arrest warrant was an odious legal document used in Old England to curb free speech. It was issued by the secretary of state, and without naming anyone the warrant authorized the arrest of printers, publishers, and writers of any documents considered libelous by the government.

Forty-eight people were snatched by the king's police on the *North Briton* warrant including John Wilkes. When Wilkes was served he suggested that since there were no names on the warrant, the police should arrest the lord high chancellor or the secretary of state. But it was Wilkes that was hauled off to the Tower, and then the king's thugs broke into his home and took every paper in the place hoping to connect Wilkes with *North Briton* No. 45.

The arrest made Wilkes an overnight hero both in England and the colonies. London mobs took to the streets shouting, "Wilkes and Liberty," and according to Ben Franklin they painted the number 45 on every house and carriage within fifteen miles of the city. A frustrated king looked to his courts to finish Wilkes off, but that was not to be. King George not only lost his court battle, but he lost so badly that the cases became legal landmarks. The Wilkes decisions outlawed the general warrant and formed the bases of modern search and seizure law in England and America.

When Wilkes was released from the Tower, he went posthaste to a magistrate and asked for the arrest of Lord Halifax, the secretary of state who had issued the general warrant. When the request was denied he wrote Halifax saying, "Your Lordship, my house has been robbed and I am informed that the stolen goods are in your possession. Please return my property." Not surprisingly, Lord Halifax ignored the letter, so Wilkes sued him and was awarded four thousand pounds from a London jury.

Although a great champion of the poor and the oppressed, Wilkes was no saint. He was as much rascal as patriot. In a one year period he was elected to and expelled from the Parliament four times and his reputation as a womanizer was national scandal. Parliament once declared him an outlaw and he spent several years hiding on the Continent. But he returned to England as a hero and was named lord mayor of London.

Colonial Americans were so proud of John Wilkes that they named their cities and children in his honor. But John Wilkes Booth ended that tradition; it's a sad irony that someone named after that great British champion of human rights should tarnish that name by assassinating a great American champion of human rights.

The crucifixion of Jesus Christ marked the end of two of the greatest courtroom dramas of all time. The picture of a Roman governor washing his hands before an angry crowd and sending Christ off to die is known to all. But before Jesus appeared in that Roman court, he was first tried by the Great Sanhedrin of the Jewish religious community.

Judea during the time of Christ was under the strict control of Rome. Pontius Pilate served as Caesar's procurator or governor and held a tight reign on the legal system. No death sentence could be carried out without his approval and most legal matters were reserved for the Roman courts. But as a small boon the conquerors permitted their Jewish subjects to conduct their own religious courts. These Hebrew religious courts were divided into three tiers and the highest, located in Jerusalem, was called the Great Sanhedrin. Caiaphas, the Jewish High Priest, served as the presiding judge of this seventy-one member court.

Jewish law did not permit the Great Sanhedrin to try anyone at night or on Friday or on the Feast of the Passover. The court also had a rule that any unanimous verdict of guilty on the day of trial had the effect of an acquittal. But so intense were the passions regarding the Nazarene that rules were broken.

Jesus was taken on Thursday night from the garden of Gethsemane and appeared before the Great Sanhedrin as quickly as a quorum could be assembled. He was accused of blasphemy, and Caiaphas prosecuted the case. The evidence was thin and the trial was not going well for the accusers. Finally, according to St. Mark, the judge asked Jesus, "Art thou the Christ?" and when Jesus answered, "I am," Caiaphas stood, ripped his garment and proclaimed Jesus guilty.

Jewish tradition required that one's tunic be torn the length of the palm of the hand in the presence of a blasphemer and had a majority of the judges done the same, Jesus would have been convicted. Pilate would have rubber stamped the verdict and approved the death penalty. But death would have been by stoning or strangulation or decapitation, the traditional Jewish methods. Although the colleagues of Caiaphas could not agree Jesus was guilty of blasphemy, they all agreed he was worthy of death, so he was taken to the court of the Roman procurator for a second trial.

Caiaphas presented Christ as the man from Galilee who would be king; the mention of Galilee was no accident. That area was notorious for anti-Roman activity. The Zealots of Galilee once led a countrywide uprising against Roman rule that ended with two thousand Jews on the cross and another twenty thousand sold into slavery. The chief priest knew the mention of Galilee would weigh heavily against Jesus.

Pilate asked if Jesus was the King of the Jews, and Christ answered, "Thou sayest." Pilate, a brutal but cowardly bureaucrat, would take no chances with this potential revolutionary. What was the life of one Jew— particularly one disliked even by his own people.

So, with the washing of his hands, Pilate sent the man from Galilee to Calvary to await his Crucifixion—the Roman punishment for political crimes—and the two trials of Jesus Christ came to their tragic end. The son of a carpenter who brought his people a message of peace and lived by the law of love was to die at the hands of those whose hate obscured their traditional sense of both love and law.

≈

The old adage, "It's better that ten guilty persons go free than one innocent person should suffer," is one of the best known maxims of American law. It's at the very heart of our criminal justice system and is as American as Mom's apple pie. But that famous quote didn't come from any of the men meeting in Philadelphia's Independence Hall. It was a gift from Sir William Blackstone, a loyal Tory who probably would have fought for the king had he lived in the colonies.

Blackstone was an eighteenth-century English superstar. He was an architect, poet, businessman, and writer. He was knighted by the king, named judge of the common pleas court, elected to Parliament, and was the first professor to teach the common law in the history of England. But this legal and academic giant, who molded the young minds of England's upper crust, was born a commoner. Both parents died before he was thirteen and he became known as the orphan of Cheapside. But like a Horatio Alger hero, he rose from obscurity and poverty to hold a position of wealth and importance in English society and unwittingly played a key role in the American Revolution.

Blackstone was appointed to Oxford's new chair of English common law in 1758 and it was here that he began a lecture series that would make him famous. Those Oxford lectures were published in a work titled *Commentaries on the Laws of England,* and with the exception of the Bible probably no other book has had a greater impact on the social history of America.

Blackstone's *Commentaries* provided the first important outline of common law principles. The publication's timing was perfect for the restless settlers of New England. It gave rebel leaders legal ammunition in their battle with the English king, and after independence, the work was used to help determine what portions of English law would be preserved by the new republic.

The *Commentaries* became the chief, if not the only lawbooks of the American lawyer and the chief textbooks for American students of law. More copies of Blackstone's *Commentaries* were sold in America than in England. They became a sort of do-it-yourself manual for the development of the legal system in backwoods America. For many a struggling lawyer or judge, a volume of Blackstone was both the law school and the law library.

It is one of the great paradoxes of history that Blackstone, a staunch and loyal supporter of the monarchy, should give aid and comfort to the enemies of his king and play a key role in the establishment of a republican form of government in America. The revolution freed the United States from Great Britain, and thanks to Blackstone the citizens of this new republic had English common law to help preserve their liberty.

The "ten guilty persons" maxim is a minor part of Blackstone's legal legacy. His *Com-*

mentaries still tell citizens of both nations that liberty is the best birthright and noblest inheritance of mankind, and they remind us yet today of our need to protect and defend liberty if we are to leave that legacy to others.

Benedict Arnold was probably the greatest fighting general in the service of the Continental army. In fact, he served the struggling new nation both as a general and an admiral, and his courage and military leadership were critical to the early success of the revolution. But he lives in history as America's best known traitor and is one on a long list of those convicted of the world's most universally condemned crime. Although Arnold is America's most famous traitor, he was not the first. That distinction goes to a counterfeiter named Thomas Hickey.

In June 1776, the Provincial Congress discovered a ring of counterfeiters. The bogus money was being used to recruit a pro-British armed force in the State of New York. Thomas Hickey, a soldier and member of General George Washington's personal guard, was part of the counterfeiting plot. General Washington quickly convened a court martial. Hickey was tried for treason under the nation's new Articles of War and was convicted. He died on the gallows within twenty-four hours after his trial.

Every nation has suffered the shock and embarrassment of treason and espionage at one time or another. Our neighbors to the north were stunned in 1945 when a Soviet embassy cypher clerk exposed a network of Canadians operating as spies. Dr. Claus Fuchs, the British physicist, sold his nation's atomic power secrets to the Communists, and British morale was devastated in 1962 when the treason of the "Cambridge Four" was discovered. That group included the famous Kim Philby who was a top ranking British intelligence officer. Unfortunately, Philby was a double agent who passed the most sensitive of British secrets to his Soviet spy master.

While today's journalists talk of the Walker spy case, the press in the 1950s reported the espionage story of Ethel and Julius Rosenberg. After their convictions for wartime espionage, they became the nation's first nonmilitary citizens to be executed for treason.

Historically, death has been the usual penalty for a traitor. As far back as 450 B.C. the Roman law of the Twelve Tablets promised death to those who gave aid to the enemy. But traditionally there has been a division between high and petty treason. High treason involved armed rebellion or an attack on the sovereign and always called for death. In the early Middle Ages, a person convicted of high treason was literally dragged to the execution tied to the tail of a horse. The rope or ax was used to eliminate male traitors while females were burned at the stake.

For petty treason, the pillory was a frequent punishment, with the traitor's ears nailed to the wooden frame. Sometimes the traitor's ears were cut off, and those who spoke against the king had part of their tongue cut off. Whipping was another punishment but was for men only. The pillory could be used for either sex, while the ducking stool was exclusively for women.

Treason has always been considered an outrage and is the one crime specifically written into our Constitution. But the American definition of treason is centuries older than the republic itself, and the words used paraphrase those of the statute of treason passed by the British Parliament in 1354.

Patrick Henry captured the imagination of early Americans with his cry for liberty or death, but Henry Ward Beecher expressed the nation's disgust with treason when he said, "A traitor is a good fruit to hang from the boughs of the tree of liberty."

On October 7, 1949, an American woman was sentenced to ten years in prison and fined ten thousand dollars for treason. Her name was Ikuko Toguri. But to the soldiers and sailors who fought World War II in the Pacific she was Tokyo Rose.

Ikuko Toguri was the American-born daughter of Japanese immigrants; she was raised in southern California and educated at UCLA. In July 1941, she was sent to Japan to help care for an ailing aunt, but she stayed too long and when the Japanese attacked Pearl Harbor, Ikuko found herself on the wrong side of the Pacific.

She refused to renounce her American citizenship, so the Japanese classified her as an enemy alien. She survived on a part-time news agency job monitoring English language broadcasts until 1943 when she landed a typing job at Radio Tokyo. It was there that she met some American POW's working on a new English language program to be called "Zero Hour."

The "Zero Hour" needed a woman's voice and Ikuko was asked to read scripts. So Ikuko Toguri took to the airwaves. She called herself Orphan Annie, but the fighting men of the Pacific called her Tokyo Rose. The Japanese hoped the "Zero Hour" would demoralize the allied troops, but most found the program a welcome relief. The husky voice of Tokyo Rose was fun to hear and there was always humor in the news reports. An American bomber is even said to have parachuted a carton of new pop tunes over Tokyo to help update the station's record library.

When the war ended, two Hurst reporters went looking for Tokyo Rose. In reality, the "Zero Hour" used a number of female voices and Ikuko was just one of them. But they found Ikuko and offered $2,000 for her story. The check was never issued, but an arrest warrant was. Ikuko was locked in Sugamo Prison along with Tojo and the Japanese war criminals and for nearly a year held without charges, bail, or trial. Then she was released.

Ikuko wanted to return home and applied for her American passport. When the press reported that Tokyo Rose would return to Amer-

ica, the public went wild. "Hang the traitor" was the cry and Ikuko was arrested again and indicted on eight counts of treason. For two years she sat in prison waiting for trial. When the prosecution began there was little evidence of any treason, but the name Tokyo Rose was too much to overcome and a reluctant jury finally convicted her on one count. Ikuko served ten years in prison. The ten thousand dollars was paid by forcing her to cash in a life insurance policy and attaching her inheritance when her father died.

As the years passed and the passions of war waned, the American people took a second look at Ikuko Toguri. The California legislature passed a unanimous resolution asking President Gerald Ford for her pardon. San Francisco, Los Angeles, and Honolulu followed suit and in January 1977, Ford pardoned Ikuko Toguri and restored her citizenship.

Sometimes when we pluck a rose in haste or anger, we injure ourselves on the thorns. While it's hard to believe that Ikuko Toguri didn't know she was playing a role in Japan's propaganda war effort, the vicious prosecution and questionable trial tactics paint a sad picture, particularly since no others involved were ever charged. By the way, Ikuko Toguri was not only born in the U.S.A., but she was born on the Fourth of July.

On March 13, 1963, the Phoenix police arrested an uneducated twenty-three-year-old indigent and charged him with the crimes of kidnapping and rape. The defendant was placed in a lineup at police headquarters where an eighteen-year-old woman identified him as the man who had driven her into the desert and raped her.

Police questioned the defendant, who at first denied any involvement in the crime. But after two hours he finally admitted his guilt and even prepared a written statement outlining the details of the abduction and rape. No physical force was used to get the confession and no promises were made. Conviction came easy for the Arizona prosecutor and the case was classified as routine. But the defendant's name was Ernesto Miranda and the case was soon to become one of the most famous in American legal history.

In 1966, three years after his arrest, the U.S. Supreme Court, in a five to four decision, said that Ernesto Miranda had been denied his constitutional protections when police questioned him without advising him of his right to remain silent. The conviction was overturned and the decision sent shock waves through the law and order establishment. The Miranda decision became a major political issue of the 1968 presidential campaign.

The holding of the Supreme Court was that no statements made by a defendant could be used as evidence if the defendant had not been first told that he had a right to remain silent, that any statement made could be used against him, that he had a right to have an attorney present, and that if he was indigent an attorney would be appointed. The court said the privilege against self-incrimination was meant to protect the ignorant as well as the knowledgeable. Chief Justice Earl Warren delivered the opinion saying that the "Fifth Amendment is fundamental to our system." He noted further that advising a defendant that the right exists is so simple a procedure that courts must insist it be done.

Then came a mighty roar from the nation's police. Law enforcement would be crippled, they cried, and the criminals would run amok. The court had tied the policeman's hands, they felt, and was being overprotective of the rights of the criminal. But time passed and the Miranda warnings became a routine part of police practice. The fear that the crooks would conquer the world faded. Although the confession rate dropped, the conviction rate remained about the same. In fact, the conviction rate increased in some cities as police became more thorough in their criminal investigations.

The controversy over the Miranda decision continues however, and with today's more conservative Supreme Court some feel the days of the Miranda warnings are numbered. As for Ernesto Miranda, he would have been better off to have stayed in jail. He was retried for the kidnapping and rape—this time without his confession. But he told his girlfriend of his guilt when she visited him in jail and she testified against him at trial. In 1967, a jury convicted him a second time. In December 1972, Miranda was paroled and three years later he was killed in a barroom brawl over a card game. In his pockets, police found two wallet-sized cards that had the Miranda warning printed on them. Ironically, the police read from one of the cards found on Miranda's body to advise his suspected murderers of their constitutional rights.

Several centuries before Charlie Chan began numbering his American-born sons, the people of China were numbering the gangsters sent to the scaffold by an earlier Chinese detective. This oriental gumshoe of ancient days was named Dee. But he was Judge Dee, a respected district magistrate working in the provinces of Imperial China.

The English and American magistrates of today have limited jurisdiction and authority, but the magistrates of seventh-century China were major executives of local government with awesome powers, and Judge Dee was celebrated as a famous detective and a great statesman.

Robert Van Gulik fictionalized the exploits of Judge Dee in works titled *The Monkey and the Tiger*, and *The Chinese Nail Murders*. Van Gulik's stories offer a fascinating description of Judge Dee's wit and wisdom. The fictional yarns are exciting mysteries and provide insight into early Chinese society and its legal system.

But Judge Dee was more than just an interesting character of Van Gulik's fiction. He was real. He was born in A.D. 630 and his true adventures are recorded in the T'ang Dynasty Chronicles. Magistrate Dee was a combination judge, prosecutor, and grand jury. He commanded the police, interrogated witnesses, presided over the trial, and took care to see that sentences were properly executed.

When the magistrate traveled, a military escort guarded his person; the magistrate's compound housed the office of the coroner, was headquarters for the local militia, contained a prison and courthouse and the offices of local government.

The law in China developed as an instrument of the state. It wasn't used to protect the people from the government but rather the government from the people. As a result, citizens were afraid of the law, and the legal system was something to be avoided. Everyone thus bowed and scraped in the presence of the magistrate. Once a frightened witness was brought to the magistrate's court. He immediately dropped to his knees and began banging his head on the floor. Judge Dee looked down and said, "Let's just skip the formalities." And to think folks complain today about just standing when the judge arrives!

The Judicial Duel and Other Strange Procedures

Of all the parts of trial procedure, cross-examination has most fascinated and frightened the American public.

Mention the word *cross-examination* to someone headed for a courtroom and he'll probably turn a little green. That's because the word conjures up a movie or television image of a trial scene. Most of us have watched at least one episode of *Perry Mason*. Nobody in history cross-examined quite as successfully as that fictional lawyer. In almost every episode either a witness confessed or somebody in the back of the courtroom jumped up and admitted committing the murder. Poor old Hamilton Berger, the prosecutor, struggled with Perry for years and never did win a case.

A confession certainly helps solve some of the trial problems, but it really doesn't happen very often. If the truth were known, nine out of ten attorneys are more frightened than the witnesses about cross-examination and more attorneys than witnesses are done in by the process. In all my years as a prosecutor, defense lawyer, and judge, no one has ever confessed in the courtroom.

Trial lawyers will tell you that the work is tough and most trials are slow, tedious, often boring, and only rarely exciting. A timely confession would sure help pick up the pace, but waiting for a confession is a pretty dangerous trial tactic. Of course, every once in a while, someone does confess.

In his attorney days Abraham Lincoln once defended a chap named Grayson, who was charged with killing one Mr. Lockwood. Grayson's guilt seemed pretty certain with an eyewitness named Sovine as the state's key witness. Sovine said he had been with Lockwood when he was shot. The murder had occurred at night and Sovine said that he was twenty feet away when Grayson shot Lockwood. He said further that they were in a wooded area, that it was dark, and that the only light came from a campground about three-quarters of a mile away. But Sovine said he saw everything clearly, and could even identify the pistol because of the bright moonlight. Lincoln cross-examined. "You saw this shooting at night," Lincoln asked, "in Beach Timber, three-quarters of a mile away from the lights, saw the pistol barrel, saw the man fire, saw it twenty feet away, saw it all by moonlight?" "Yes," Sovine replied. "I told you so before."

The courtroom was quiet as Lincoln drew from his pocket an almanac, opened it to the date of the shooting, and with slow deliberation read, "On this night, the moon was unseen and did not rise until one o'clock the following morning." Lincoln then accused Sovine of the murder and Sovine, caught in his lie, finally admitted his guilt.

One of my favorite cross-examination stories involves a judge who kept interrupting a young attorney to ask questions of his own. Finally, in frustration the lawyer turned to the judge. "Your Honor," he said, "this is my first case. If you asked that question for me, I withdraw it. If you asked it for my opponent, I object to it. And, furthermore, Your Honor, if you insist on trying this case for me, for God's sake, don't lose it."

Of all the parts of trial procedure, cross-examination has most fascinated and frightened the American public. A successful cross-examination, like Lincoln's has the excitement of a knockout punch in a prize fight. But as your lawyer will advise you, you can't get hurt if you're honest and sincere and just tell the truth. Remember, truth alone is consistent with itself.

If for any reason you ever find yourself headed for a courtroom—as a plaintiff or a defendant or even as a witness—you'll probably have a bad case of the butterflies as the trial date comes close. Since going to court is not something you do everyday, you don't quite know what to expect and a little anxiety is understandable.

But, as the old saying goes, "It could be worse." In fact, it used to be a lot worse. Today if you find yourself in court accused of something, you can choose between a trial by jury or a trial by the judge. But in sixteenth-century England you would have had a more difficult choice to make. A defendant back then had to decide between a trial by battle or a trial by ordeal, and both were rather risky.

Trial by battle was probably the more glamorous way to settle a dispute. We've all seen movies with the knights in shining armor who sat on sleek horses holding long lances waiting for the judge to drop the gauntlet so the battle could begin. The judge's job was really rather easy—whoever died lost!

Even though trial by battle was exciting and glamorous, it was obviously dangerous and could be expensive. Not many folks had horses that could charge very far or often with four hundred pounds of armor on its back; the armor itself was hard and costly and difficult to come by. So most ordinary people had to settle for trial by ordeal.

After a trial by ordeal was decided upon, the next step in the old trial practice was to select the particular ordeal. The three most common were ordeals by morsel, fire, or water.

For the fire ordeal, the defendant could walk over hot coals, stick an arm into boiling water, or have a hot poker pressed into the palm of his hand. The burns were then medicated and wrapped. Three days later the wrappings were removed and an official checked the burned area. If the sores were healing it was a sign from God of innocence. If not, the verdict was guilty and it was off to the nearest tree where a sturdy rope was used to relieve the misery.

People weren't too crazy about the fire ordeal, but the water ordeal wasn't much better. Here the judges and citizens would take the accused, bind him with rope, and drop him into some nearby river or stream. Now, here's the strange part. If the person drowned, he was innocent! The idea was that

if the defendant sank, the water had received him, meaning he was pure of heart. Of course, not everybody drowned; it depended on how fast the court personnel could pull the individual up. All in all, however, still a risky trial choice.

The most popular of the ordeals was the ordeal by morsel. In this ordeal the accused would swallow feathers or eat bread crusts. If he could keep the feathers down or not choke on the crusts that was a signal of innocence. Not real tasty, but relatively safe.

American trial practice has changed considerably since it began its development in sixteenth-century England. Today's courts may be a little slow, but the greatest ordeal is the risk that the lawyers may talk too much or bore you to death. No one's drowned lately at a trial, and all things considered, it's certainly an improvement over the trials of yesteryear.

Every few years, following some sensational crime, Americans go through a period of national soul searching regarding our criminal justice system. We look at the way we handle the accused; and, more often than not, we take a hard look at the so-called insanity defense. John Hinckley's attempt to assassinate President Reagan was one such event, and his acquittal, by reason of insanity, sparked heated debate throughout the nation.

Historically, the insanity defense was born from an attempted assassination in Great Britain. The defense didn't officially exist before 1800 when a war injured, former British soldier named James Hadfield took a shot at King George III. His lawyer successfully argued that Hadfield had a deranged mind caused by his war injuries. The jury found Hadfield not guilty, but added to the verdict their belief that he was under the influence of insanity at the time the act was committed. The defendant was whisked off to an asylum until His Majesty's pleasures be known. Since

this was the same His Majesty that Hadfield had tried to shoot, no one will be surprised to hear that Hadfield stayed in that asylum until he died.

A few years later, a chap named Daniel M'Naghten attempted to assassinate Sir Robert Peel, the British prime minister, but he killed the leader's private secretary instead. When a jury acquitted M'Naghten based on insanity, the public was outraged. The judges of England were summoned to the House of Lords to answer questions concerning the insanity defense. The answers became known as the M'Naghten Rule, and said that a defendant would not legally be responsible for his actions if he either did not know the nature of his conduct or realize his actions were wrong. That test was imported to America and has been used by most states at one time or another.

Following the Hinckley trial, another indignant public questioned the insanity defense. People understood that Hinckley was insane but were frightened by the possibility he would soon be back on the streets. Unlike Hadfield, who died in the asylum, those acquitted today may never see a jail or hospital. A new insanity defense for use in federal and state courts seems essential if the judicial system is to retain public confidence—a defense that protects the public as well as the accused.

But when we review the insanity defense, let's keep things in perspective. It is used in no more than 2 percent of all criminal cases and is unsuccessful most of the time. The crazies are really not running rampant through the streets, and it's not time to push the panic button.

The Hinckley acquittal focused attention on a new verdict called guilty but mentally ill. If a defendant pleads not guilty by reason of insanity, the guilty but mentally ill verdict would be automatically submitted to the jury. Although popular, that verdict presents some problems. It offers an easy compromise for a jury, but a verdict of guilty but mentally ill means about as much as guilty but bald. The practical effect is that the defendant has been found guilty and will ride off on the same bus headed for the same penitentiary as any other criminal. It does not mandate treatment. It satisfies the public anxiety and keeps the defendant off the street. But it also changes some fundamental principles of justice.

Given the inability of the psychiatric community to say with certainty that a defendant is truly cured, the guilty but mentally ill verdict may be what we want. But let's not be hoodwinked into thinking it solves our problems with the mentally disturbed. What's on the label should be what's in the box, which is not true for the verdict guilty but mentally ill.

When the police broke into the Kansas City home of Fremont Weeks in 1911, a legal battle began that is still being fought. The police found evidence during their search that convicted Weeks of a federal crime, but there was one problem—the police had had no search warrant. The Supreme Court overturned the Weeks case in 1914 saying the search violated the defendant's Fourth Amendment rights. Nobody paid much attention to the case. The ruling involved only federal courts and most police cases were in the state courts. But the case was the birth of the so-called Exclusionary Rule.

In 1957, the Exclusionary Rule of the Weeks case reached full bloom. In May of that year a dozen Cleveland police officers who were looking for a bombing suspect surrounded the home of Dolly Mapp. Although Dolly said no, the police went in, handcuffed her to the banister and searched her home. They found no bomber, but Dolly did have a trunk full of dirty pictures. Ohio modesty was shocked and Dolly was convicted on a pornography charge. But there was one problem—the police had had no search warrant.

So it was back to the Supreme Court, which decided "to close courtroom doors to evidence secured by official lawlessness." The Exclusionary Rule would henceforth apply to state courts. Prosecutors and police throughout the nation let out a mighty roar. Surely, now the criminals would rule the world.

The theory of the Supreme Court was simple. Our Constitution intended to protect certain freedoms and the Fourth Amendment was to keep us safe from unreasonable searches and seizures. The Exclusionary Rule would force authorities to respect the Constitution. There would be no incentive for police to break into a home if what was found couldn't be used as evidence.

But if the Court thought the problem was solved, it was wrong. Everyone can cite at least one horror story of a crook that got off by a technicality, and there are still grim reports about police misconduct. A 1978 General Accounting Office study said that only .04 percent of federal cases were rejected because of the Exclusionary Rule. Yet a 1982 National Institute of Justice study said that nearly 5 percent of the felony arrests in California were rejected because of the rule. So the effect of the ruling is uncertain.

We know the pendulum of the clock swings in two directions, and in June 1984 the Burger Supreme Court gave us some exceptions to the rule. One case involved a man accused of rape and assault with a weapon. The police chased him into an all-night A & P, caught him, and asked where he had hid the gun. But the police questioned the suspect before reading him the Miranda warnings, so the New York courts excluded the gun from being used as evidence. This time the prosecution appealed and the Supreme Court said that it was okay to question a suspect before he is warned of his rights if the inquiry is prompted by concern for public safety. In another case the Court said that evidence improperly obtained could be used if proper discovery was inevitable. Then it was the civil libertarians turn to let out a mighty roar, claiming that America would now surely become a fascist police state.

The police hail the new ruling as a return to common sense; the civil libertarians cry that freedom is dead. I suspect the death reports are premature. A look at the Exclusionary

Rule's seventy-year history, shows that the criminals have never taken over; the jails remain full, and police procedures have never been better. Ten years from now my bet is we'll see the country did not become a police state, the courts will still be protecting individual rights, the jails will still be full, and, of course, people will still be arguing about the Exclusionary Rule.

When Congress passed the Volstead Act in October 1919, it was seen as the second part of the law's one-two punch sending John Barleycorn to the grave. Volstead was the six-term Minnesota congressman whose legislation would implement the Constitution's new Eighteenth Amendment. Prohibition was to be the law of the land and the Volstead Act would help the Anti-Saloon League save America from the evils of whiskey and beer.

As a moral exercise, Prohibition was termed a "noble experiment." But as an exercise in the law it was a disaster. The Volstead Act and the Eighteenth Amendment gave America its roaring twenties and filled the history books with countless pages of nostalgia. Big Bill Thompson and Al Capone, speakeasies and the Cotton Club, Elliott Ness and the Untouchables are all part of the era's mystique.

But the fun, excitement, and glamour of the popular image paint a different picture than the facts of reality. Prohibition brought organized crime to America and institutionalized corruption. During the law's thirteen short years of existence, liquor agents shot and killed 1,365 people while hundreds more died

in the work-a-day world of the gangsters. The Justice Department doubled its operating budget, doubled the money spent in prison maintenance, and tripled the number of federal prison inmates. The price of a beer went from 10 cents to 80 cents; a bottle of whiskey from $1.70 to $7.00, and gin went from less than a dollar to $6.00 a fifth.

The illegal bars of old Ireland, called speak softly shops, spread across America like a fire storm under their new name "speakeasy." And the speakeasy served America its first cocktail, a concoction designed to hide the terrible taste of converted industrial alcohol by mixing it with the soft drinks of the time.

Sacramental wines, which were legal, did a booming business and bathtub gin became the national craze. The pre-prohibition breweries pleaded unsuccessfully with Congress for legislation permitting the sale of beer for medicinal purposes. Anheuser-Busch spent $18 million converting its plant to the production of near beer, but quit making the brew because it couldn't compete with the illegal sale of real beer.

By 1928 Prohibition had become a divisive American political issue. It pitted the big city voters against the rural folks. Al Smith owes his presidential defeat in part to his support of the "wet" issue, while Hoover made commitments to both sides.

One of President Hoover's first acts was to appoint a Commission on Law Observance and Enforcement to make recommendations on Prohibition. And one of his first problems was finding someone willing to chair that group. After several refusals, a former attorney general named George Wickersham was finally named chairman, and after months of bitter infighting the commission issued its report.

Humorist Frank McKinney Hubbard took a look at the report and quipped, "All I can get out o' the Wickersham position on prohibition is that the distinguished jurist seems to feel that if we'd let 'em have it, the problem o' keeping 'em from getting it would be greatly simplified."

Although Prohibition remained through the Hoover years, it was the Depression, not the government, that closed speakeasies. When the "noble experiment" was finally laid to rest by F.D.R. in 1933, old John Barleycorn and his disciples marched to the funeral. To the great chagrin of the Anti-Saloon League, on the day Prohibition died, America had 23 percent more speakeasies than they had taverns before Prohibition had begun.

For years Mickey Mouse and Donald Duck were favorite write-in candidates of mischievous voters. But in the machine age, voters pull a lever or punch a card to vote. Computers may in dull fact count the votes faster, but punch cards just don't have the color or mystique of the ballots of yesteryear.

It wasn't too long ago that folks voted with corn and beans. A hat was passed and if you were for something you dropped in a kernel of corn. If you were against it you dropped in a bean. The problem was that some rogue was always dropping in an extra bean or two. So the bean ballots gave way to the bullet ballots. Bullets were painted red for yes, white for no, and one of each was given to voters. Folks dropped the bullet of their choice in a box. If they didn't like the outcome of the election, the leftover bullet came in handy for encouraging a recount!

The changes over the years in the way we vote reflect the legal system's struggle to make elections honest. At first people voted by voice or a show of hands. But then everyone knew how their neighbors voted and that created problems. So people began to vote with things—beans, bullets, seashells, paper ballots, and finally machines.

The word *ballot* comes from the Italian word *ballotta* which describes a little ball used for secret voting. The ballot was first used by Greek judges in the fifth century B.C. They voted with colored balls or seashells or with stones painted black for guilty or white for acquittal.

For several centuries voters came to the voting place with a scroll or piece of paper and wrote out their own ballots by hand. But then a Massachusetts candidate decided to print his name on paper strips and pass them out to voters. The election was challenged, but the state court held that his printed ballot was okay. Political parties got into the act and started printing party ballots. They were called party strips but looked like railroad tickets and so came the phrase "voting the ticket." Candidates had to pay to have their names on the strips and the ballots were printed on bright colored paper. That brought the White Paper Ballot law to regulate both the size and color of ballots.

The Australians were the first to use the "X." Until 1877, the voters scratched out the names of candidates they didn't want. But the government finally decided it was easier for people to mark an "X" by the name of the candidate they did want. The Australians were also the first to print ballots at government expense for voters. That system was called the Australian ballot and was later adopted throughout the United States.

Today's election process might be a little pale by comparison, but we've come a long way since the bean and bullet days. Reformers tell us that elections are now more open and honest and they're probably right. It's tough on Mickey and Donald, but write-in voters shouldn't despair. American ingenuity will find some way to elect the Disney team. Just look around, maybe somewhere they already have!

George Orwell proclaimed 1984 as the year of Big Brother. By that year the eyes of an evil government would be watching our every move. Fortunately, 1984 wasn't as bad as Orwell predicted, although some feel it came close. But long before Orwell told us what Big Brother could do, the monarchs of Old England were doing it. In the United States, the real government of 1984 and beyond is

friendly by comparison, and in many ways we never had it so good.

From the fourteenth century on, English kings regulated almost every aspect of the citizen's life—including the fashion of his clothing, the number of courses he could serve for dinner, and how many guests he could have at a wedding. King Edward III was called the king who taught the English how to dress, and he used a series of laws, called sumptuary laws, to regulate the lifestyle of his people. Silk, for example, could be worn only by the upper classes; lace was forbidden on the clothes of the poor; it was a crime to serve more than two courses for dinner or for women to paint their faces or wear counterfeit jewelry.

The sumptuary laws were part of English life for over four hundred years, but they reached their zenith during the reign of Elizabeth I. Imported clothing was forbidden and every male over six was required to wear an English cap of wool on Sundays and holidays. No one under the rank of knight's son was permitted to wear a velvet cap and lords of the manor were to check servants' apparel to make sure they had no contraband clothing. These laws were intended to stop waste and extravagance, but Elizabeth's personal wardrobe numbered more than two thousand dresses and she exempted her friends from the laws. Of course, the English woolen and clothing industry thought these laws were the cat's pajamas—English woolen pajamas, naturally!

It was illegal for men to wear cloth containing gold or silver or any purple colored silk unless the man was at least an earl. Foreign wool was illegal unless you were a baron, and women couldn't wear anything with velvet unless they were at least the wife of a knight. Violation of a sumptuary law could cost you a fine and sometimes get you in jail.

In 1536, King Henry ordered the poor Irish to shave their upper lips and let their hair grow until it covered their ears. Speech was regulated and the House of Commons passed an act making it a crime to curse or swear. First offense swearing for dukes, viscounts, or barons was thirty shillings. For baronets it was twenty shillings, and for a gentleman six shillings. Peasants paid only three shillings a curse. Recreation was also regulated; if it was fun, it was probably prohibited.

By the time the American colonies took root, sumptuary laws had disappeared in England. Still, they found a way into the New England legislation. Rules against using silk or gold in clothing were approved, and an order in 1636 prohibited the sale of lace to the poor. But in the great tradition of independent Americans, the colonists wanted no part of importing the tyrannies of English monarchs, and so far we have avoided the predicted tyrannies of Orwell's Big Brother. But eternal vigilance is the price of freedom and we should remember Edmond Burke's famous line, "The best way for evil to triumph is for good men to do nothing."

There are over five hundred thousand lawyers in the United States serving a population of about two hundred million people. China, a country with over eight hundred million people, has probably fewer than five thousand lawyers. Yet, the Chinese Empire had a well-developed bureaucracy and was using law to regulate society more than a thousand years before the birth of Christ. The Chinese legal system was in operation centuries before the white wigged judges of Old England held court in Westminster Palace. But before you lawyers start packing your bags, there are some other things you should know. .

The difference in numbers reflects a difference in philosophy and purpose. The law in China developed as an instrument of the state. It wasn't used to protect the people from the government but rather the government from the people. As a result, citizens were afraid of the law and the legal system was something to be avoided.

A number of Chinese proverbs reflect the general distrust of the legal system. One says, "Of ten reasons by which a judge may decide a case, nine are known only to the magistrate." Another, "Win your lawsuit and lose your money." And a third quotes Confucius saying, "In hearing cases I am as good as anyone else, but what is really needed is to bring about that there are no cases."

If you and your neighbor in China had an argument you didn't sue; instead, you went to the local magistrate who decided whether or not to prosecute. There was no private legal profession to help with your lawsuit. Some people were available to help prepare a legal petition—for a fee—and these early lawyers were called litigation tricksters. But they were regarded as troublemakers and in 1820 the Chinese emperor called them "rascally fellows who entrapped people for the sake of profit." As a result, they were often arrested and many ended up in jail. So it's no wonder there are so few lawyers in China and American lawyers who think they have an image problem can be happy they're here and not there.

Trained legal officials operated only on the very highest level of government. On the county level, the one closest to the people, the law was handled by the county magistrate as one of several administrative functions. Magistrates had almost no legal training and served also as detective, prosecutor, judge, and jury all rolled into one. Every American with a television set knows Charlie Chan. But the real detective fans also know about Judge Dee. He was an imperial Chinese magistrate who not only heard cases but solved most of them—à la Perry Mason.

The story of the lambskin coat gives us an example of the work and wisdom of the early Chinese magistrate. Around A.D. 400 a salt carrier and a wood carrier were fighting over a lambskin coat. Each claimed the coat was his. The magistrate ordered an officer to "question the skin under torture." The officer was dumbfounded. How could the lambskin answer questions? The magistrate placed the lambskin on a mat and had it beaten with a stick. As it was beaten, grains of salt came out and the wood carrier admitted his lie and begged forgiveness.

The Chinese argue that law doesn't make

society better and that written laws let people find loopholes so they can violate the law. Rulers should govern by example and virtue. An emperor who rules by law admits the loss of virtue and a breakdown of the system. Perhaps there's something to be learned from this philosophy. Our codes certainly haven't eliminated crime and, although five thousand years of virtue haven't eliminated problems in China, I think there's still something to be said for expecting our officials to govern by example and virtue as well as by law.

Since the beginning of time a chap with a few extra bob in his pockets has been able to find something to gamble it away on. The Egyptians were throwing dice two thousand years before the birth of Christ, and the forerunners of modern casino crap tables have been found buried in those ancient Egyptian tombs. Historically, gambling has ranked with prostitution and whiskey drinking as the more frustrating of society's dilemmas.

In eighteenth-century England, gambling was so widespread that when the British Parliament passed an anti-gambling act, the legislators had to add a provision which threatened to punish the judges if they ignored the new law. Today the British are still tinkering with laws to curb gambling, the success of which can be measured by the reputation of London casinos among the international high rollers.

The Old Testament tells of the wager of Samson. The Roman Justinian code made games of chance illegal. In ancient Jewish society, a person who gambled was prohibited from ever becoming a magistrate. In fact, the Jews refused to permit a gambler even to testify as a witness in court. Their philosophy held that gambling was against the public good and avarice was presumed.

Of course, not all people were prohibited from gambling—usually it was only the poor. In 1553 while Cardinal Wolsey was trying to burn all of England's playing cards and bowling pins, we find King Henry VIII losing a few quid in a dicing match.

The Chinese are credited with the introduction of playing cards to the nations of the world. Then, when folks grew tired of throwing dice for such games as passage and hazard, in and in, doublets, tic tack, Irish or backgammon, they could break out a deck of cards and enjoy a friendly game of one in thirty, poor and rich, ruffe, flam, trump, naughty, or wisk. Of course, the pièce de résistance for playing card gamblers came with the introduction of poker. That was also a gift from our Oriental cousins and was introduced to Americans in the nineteenth century.

In most ancient societies, the law considered money won by gambling as a theft. The winner couldn't sue for money owed, but a loser could recover money lost; however, no loser who sued for his money back or who skipped out on a debt was ever considered a good health risk.

Just as there is a law of physics that says for every action there is an equal and opposite reaction, there is a similar law for gambling.

For every new gambling game invented, a new way to cheat is invented. Loaded dice were found in the ruins of Pompeii, weighted coins in the gambling dens of old Rome, and the gambling museums display some of history's more ingenious ways to mark playing cards. So it's little wonder that Nevada and New Jersey, London, Monte Carlo, Hong Kong, and Nassau among others have legalized gambling. That way the government can watch for cheats—at least the tax cheats.

Gambling may or may not be legal in your hometown; either way it's almost never profitable and the best advice is don't gamble. But if you weaken one day and feel exceptionally lucky, let me share with you some words from Damon Runyon, the man who created the gambling characters of *Guys and Dolls*. He paraphrased Ecclesiastes when he said, "The race is not always to the swift or the battle to the strong—but that's the way the smart money goes!"

When William Shakespeare died, he left his wife his "second best bed." We don't know where his best bed was, or who was in it, and historians still argue about what he meant. The idea of being able to leave property to family or friends has been with us for centuries. The wall writings on Egyptian tombs were ancient wills of five thousand years ago. And Moses seems to have been talking about a bequest when he said Jacob gave Joseph a portion above his brother.

In primitive societies property was passed on to families but not because people cared about the survivors. They were afraid of the dead and believed the spirit would come back to haunt if they didn't take care of the kin. Some societies buried property with the body thinking money or a sword might be used in the afterlife. But the missionaries stopped that ritual by changing the perception of afterlife. Then property went to the family and to the church for the remission of sin. Because saving the soul became so important, priests were often named executor of wills and church courts used to enforce them.

The longest will on record was admitted to probate in 1925. It took 96,000 words on 1,100 pages in four volumes to dispose of a $100,000 estate. The smallest will was written on the identification disk of a British soldier and consisted of three words "all to mother." Wills have been written on hat boxes, hospital charts, and the walls of jail cells. One was found on an eggshell and another on a farm tractor fender. Another was part of a chili sauce menu which read, "four quarts of tomatoes, four small onions, four green peppers, two tea cups of sugar. Measure tomatoes when peeled. In case I die before my husband, I leave everything to him."

Some of the wills of history are famous because of the memorials they established. Alfred Nobel established the Nobel prize program through his will and the Rhodes scholarships were established through the will of Cecil Rhodes.

Other wills are remembered because of their humor. In 1716, an Englishman left his neighbor "one word of mine because he has never kept one of his own." Another reflected a brother's politics when he said, "I leave nothing to my two sisters, Hazel and Catherine, as they revere Franklin D. Roosevelt and the taxes caused by him more than equal their share." A New York tailor died with seventy-one pairs of trousers in his shop. He ordered them sold without examination, one to a customer. When the buyers opened the pocket stitching, they found each contained a thousand dollars.

Of course, not all wills bring joy, and husband and wife quarrels provide us with some of history's more vindictive wills. In a one-liner that says it all, a husband wrote, "To my wife Anna (who is no good) I leave a dollar." Another left his wife a schilling saying she picked the rest of his estate out of his pants' pockets while he was alive.

Most husbands leave funds for their spouse, but often say she should be cut off if she remarries. On the other hand, a New York governor who married a younger woman left her a handsome income with the provision that if she remarried the income would double. With less love, a German poet left his wife all his assets on the condition that she remarry. He said then there'd be at least one man around to regret his death.

Of course, there's nothing funny when survivors fight over the property and it happens too often. So it's best to plan your estate, prepare a will, and do it with professional help. Maybe you can't take it with you, but if you'll take a little time, you can still have fun with your funds—even when you're gone!

When Shakespeare's Juliet asked, "What's in a name?" and said, "That which we call a rose / By any other word would smell as sweet," she was trying to point out that the name does not make the person. In name Romeo, because he was a Montague, was her enemy; but the person of Romeo she loved. For better or worse, the name is a symbol of a person's identity—at least of a man's identity.

For centuries society demanded that its women discard that identity when they married. In the English common law a husband and wife became one person through marriage. The legal existence of the woman was suspended and incorporated with the husband. The married man and woman would use only one name, the husband's. Marriage laws and custom robbed a woman of her name and identity, but one of the glories of the common law is its ability to shift with the times and in 1855, Lucy Stone set about to make a new marriage law. When she said, "My name is Lucy Stone and I'll keep it, thank you," she became the first woman in American history to keep her maiden name after marriage, and she began the development of a modern marriage custom. For many years following, married women who retained their birth name were called Lucy Stoners; and in 1921 the Lucy Stone League was formed to promote the legal right of married women to keep their maiden names.

So times change and so does the law. Today the wife has regained her legal identity. She can buy and sell property, sign her own contracts, and as long as there's no intent to defraud, she can call herself by any name she wishes without taking legal action. No state in the Union now requires a woman to use her husband's name. When Suzie Jones marries Michael Smith she can stay Suzie Jones. Or she can become Suzie Smith, Suzie Jones Smith or Suzie Jones-Smith.

Under common law names are determined by usage and people can use any name they choose as long as they do so consistently. And if children come, the couple can give them any name they wish. There's no legal requirement that a child carry either the father's or mother's last name.

But that doesn't mean there aren't problems. The bureaucrats don't like two name households. Sometimes driver's license bureaus or car title folks say you can't use your new hyphenated name. Well, they're wrong. Be pleasant but be firm! More serious problems come with tax bureaus, Social Security, and credit departments. Make sure tax and Social Security people know the old and new names so your accounts will reflect all payments.

A single woman with established credit jeopardizes that credit rating when she charges and buys under a new name. She's starting from scratch and may have the usual new credit problems. And it's never a good idea for the wife to buy or charge as Mrs. Michael Smith. The use of Mrs. Suzie Smith, for example, will help her maintain a personal credit line.

Men, of course, can also adopt the wife's name if they choose or can agree to use the hyphenated new name. Most brides, however, still elect to use their husband's name and there's certainly nothing wrong in doing so. But if you're a modern bride who elects a more novel name change, you'd better carry a large dosage of patience around with you. Remember the concept is only 130 years old. And when your frustration level reaches the boiling point, remember the words of Martin Luther King, Jr. who once told an audience, "We ain't what we oughta be; we ain't what we wanta be; we ain't what we gonna be; but thank God we ain't what we was!"

The prestigious City Club of Portland, Oregon raised the nation's eyebrows when club members recently asked city fathers to legalize prostitution. City mothers gave the request a big thumbs down, as did most women's organizations, church groups, and a few vice squad cops who feared for their jobs. Despite all the national attention, Portland's battle with prostitution is nothing new. Society and its legal systems have been waging war with prostitutes for three thousand years.

While the Star of Bethlehem guided the three wise men to Jesus, thirty-six thousand registered prostitutes worked the city of Rome. In 1189, the French Crusaders brought a shipload of prostitutes along to help reclaim the Holy Land for Christianity. In 1501, Pope Alessandro VI hired fifty prostitutes to entertain at a party. In the 1800s there were 797 registered brothels, or "stew" houses in Birmington, England, and a 1948 survey of American males showed that two out of three had used the services of a prostitute at one time or another.

Kings and princes, parliaments and councils have gone through alternate periods of frustration. First they attempt to rid society of the harlot. Then they try to regulate the business practices of the prostitutes. King Henry II set "stew" house standards in thirteenth-century England with a proclamation forbidding pimps from holding women against their will, limiting the amount of money they could take from the working girls, and insisting that no woman could take money from a man unless she spent the entire night with him—kind of a combination consumer protection act and ladies' labor law.

When government wasn't trying to regulate prostitution, it was trying to punish it. Prostitutes have been dunked, drowned, burned, beaten, and exiled. The Greeks made them wear blonde wigs and prohibited them from leaving the brothels except at night. The French and Italians made them wear red knots on their left shoulders; special clothing was a frequent requirement. Most major cities set up a special district for their licensed bordellos, common houses, abbeys, brothels, stews or clap houses.

Between efforts to rid and regulate, some noble folks tried to reform the prostitute.

These attempts were even less successful than the regulations. Sometimes they were counterproductive. A seventeenth-century French rehabilitation home was so fancy that hundreds of women turned to prostitution so that they might be eligible for reformation.

And don't let any social reformer blame the evils of prostitution on the Europeans. Years before Marco Polo came looking for silk and spice and everything nice, the Chinese were selling girls into prostitution. And long before the Europeans discovered the resources of black Africa, black African women had discovered their own resources and African brothels were doing a brisk business before Her Majesty's troops brought them VD.

So even though it was rejected, the Portland, Oregon City Club proposal to legalize and regulate prostitution was really nothing new. And when we look at history's three-thousand-year effort to regulate the world's oldest profession, it seems unlikely that the Portland proposition would have made much of an impact even if it had been approved.

Interesting Items in the Miscellaneous Column

When somebody drops an ipso facto between his res ipsa loquiturs, the odds are that somebody is a lawyer.

In 1626 a Dutchman named Peter Minuit chalked up one of the greatest real estate deals in history when he bought Manhattan Island from the Indians for a few bucks worth of junk jewelry. At least, that's the way the story goes. There's another story that says it was the Dutchman who was taken when the Indian Chief Manhasset sold Manhattan because the Indians never really owned the island. If Ralph Nader and his Raiders had been lurking around the island either the Dutchman or the Indian would have been in big trouble, because either story tells a tale of consumer fraud.

In the years since that great Manhattan Island swindle, thousands of us have fallen victim to marketplace fraud. Finally, frustrated consumers flexed their political and economic muscle and the legal system responded. The Consumer Products Warranties Act is designed to protect the American consumer from the retail tricksters, so now when you buy a stove or a TV or a toaster, the manufacturer or seller makes certain promises to you which are called warranties.

There are two kinds of warranties, express and implied, and the express warranty may be full or limited. In fact, under federal law, the item you buy must carry either a full or limited warranty. A full warranty means that if the product doesn't work it will be replaced or repaired free. Repair service must be reasonably available and be done in a reasonable time. If it can't be fixed you are entitled to a refund or a new product. Anything less than this is called a limited warranty and you must be told exactly what rights you have if the product is defective.

It is not mandatory that the warranty be in writing although most are. The warranty may be explained orally, but if it is in writing, it must be in plain, easy to understand English. That means no legal gobbledegook.

If the manufacturer or seller breaks his promise, the warranty is breached. Then you can go to court and demand your money back or sue for damages or demand a product that complies with the warranties. In many cases, you can do this in a small claims court without the need for a lawyer.

In addition to express warranties, you also get something called implied warranties when you buy a product. These are warranties of merchantability, fitness for a particular purpose, and of title. If you buy a toaster you expect it to toast. You don't need an express warranty that promises the toaster will toast —that's implied! If a clerk sells you a watch after you explain you plan to wear it swimming, it had better not take in water. Here you have a warranty for fitness for a particular purpose. And, of course, you expect the seller to have good title and not sell stolen property or something that already belongs to someone else.

Warranties also differ by manufacturer, so shop for warranties just like you shop for price. See how long the warranties run, what they cover, and what you must do to enforce warranty rights. You might also be on the lookout for disclaimers. Words like "as is" or "with all faults" should set off your consumer alarms. Remember, too, that despite all the consumer laws, there is no substitute for carefulness and common sense. If you do get snookered in today's marketplace the law offers help. But the old warning of caveat emptor or "let the buyer beware" is still good sound advice.

Having a child is one of the few things you can do today without buying a permit or license. But after the child arrives, there's a long line of people waiting with advice on how that new son or daughter should be raised. Psychologists, teachers, doctors, neighbors all have lists of do's and don'ts to follow. For the most part you're free to pick and choose from the lists and do whatever you think best. But some of your new responsibilities are mandatory and parents should have some idea of what their legal rights and obligations are.

First, the law requires parents to support their child. That means at least food, clothing, education, and medical care. Dad is primarily responsible for support, but mom may also have a support obligation. Criminal action can be filed against either parent or both for nonsupport of the child.

On the other hand, as the child grows he or

she has a duty to obey the parents. This means following the family rules on dating, curfews, smoking, and other social behavior. The courts regularly support parents in efforts to maintain family standards and the occasional use of a razor strop to help enforce those rules is also okay as long as parents don't go overboard. If the punishment causes real or serious harm, however, a parent will be open to a criminal charge of child abuse.

The hand that holds the bottle also holds the car keys, and all too soon junior or missy will begin to eye the family auto. But before the child gets behind the wheel, you would be wise to check the insurance policy. Most states require parents to be the sponsor when a child applies for a driver's license. If the youngster is later involved in an accident, the sponsor is liable, so mom and dad will get the bill.

But mom and dad are not responsible for contracts their children sign unless, of course, they act as cosigner. It's the merchant's decision whether or not to take a contract from a minor, and he does so at his own risk. Even if the merchant thinks your child is old enough or the child says he or she is of legal age, the parent still has no responsibility. You may have to return the merchandise, but you don't have to pay the bill.

Parents are liable for civil wrongs—called torts—committed by their child. The responsibility varies but most states limit liability to a certain amount, often four or five thousand dollars. So, if your youngster destroys some

school property or throws a brick through the neighbor's window, get ready to pay the bill.

Most parents are loving folks who try to do what's best for their child. Unfortunately, some abuse and neglect their children. When that happens the courts have both a right and obligation to place the children in a foster home or a social agency. When viewing a child neglect or abuse problem, the court uses "the best interests of the child" test. But because that's a bit vague, some courts have spelled out the specific circumstances under which a child would be taken—abandonment, for example, or parent disability resulting from alcohol, drugs, or mental illness.

There are tough legal questions involved in terminating parental rights. It's not easy, nor should it be. Both parents and children have a right to be free from government interference and natural parents have a right to the care and custody of their children. But children have a right not to be neglected or abused and the state has a responsibility to protect society's children. As John Milton reminds us in *Paradise Regained*, "The childhood shows the man, / As morning shows the day."

When E. F. Hutton speaks, everyone listens—trying to catch a word or two on the market's hot items. Jeane Dixon starts each New Year with predictions about everything from celebrity divorces to nuclear arms talks. During the football season the Ax and Jimmy the Greek predict the winners and give us the point spreads, and any day's edition of *USA Today* will give sport fans the line on everything from basketball to the National Frog Jumping Contest.

That's all pretty important stuff, but there's still a major void in predicting winners. No one's looking into his crystal ball to predict the winners of the big legal battles on the schedule of the Supreme Court. After all, the Supreme Court is the Super Bowl for lawsuits and the results are at least as important as most football games.

So, to give new life to the old adage that "fools rush in," Jerry the Judge offers his graded handicap of Supreme Court cases. This legal "tip sheet" covers the Scarsdale Christmas Creche case, the Tennessee "fleeing felon" statute, the unwanted party guest at the Air Force Open House, and the case of the Oklahoma insane indigent.

Jerry the Judge picks the Scarsdale Creche Committee to have a nativity scene on the field ready for action at the kickoff of the 1985 holiday season. When the Supreme Court justices break their huddle, the Scarsdale group will be declared the winner by a one justice spread.

Tennessee's battle to uphold its "fleeing felon" statute is rated as a pick. The state won the playoffs when lower courts said the use of deadly force to stop unarmed suspects fleeing from nonviolent felonies was okay. But the opposing team in the *Tennessee v. Garner* case has beefed up the defense with some serious constitutional ar-

guments. It's too close to call and a law clerk here could make the difference.

The whistles will blow and an unsportsmanlike conduct penalty will be assessed against officials of Hawaii's Hickham Air Force Base for their treatment of an antiwar demonstrator who came to their open house. When James Albertini accepted the public invitation to attend the Air Force party, he was charged and then convicted of a form of trespassing.

Jerry the Judge picks Albertini to win in this First Amendment contest with the Court giving him a right to attend the public open house despite his bad manners and the fact he may have been offside.

But the best bet of the 1985 card is on Ake of *Ake v. Oklahoma*. The issue here is whether the state must provide psychiatric assistance to an indigent defendant trying to establish an insanity defense. Even the toughest justice knows Ake can't call the plays without help from a coach. This could be a shut-out and the line gives Ake a three justice spread.

Now Ake may be the best bet, but the best advice from Jerry the Judge is to keep your money in your wallet. Remember the Chinese proverb that says, "Of ten ways to decide a case, nine are known only to the magistrate." Calling a sports contest is tough, but with the nine captains all calling their own plays, handicapping the Supreme Court is tougher and even Jimmy the Greek makes an occasional mistake. Of course, Jerry the

Judge is Irish, and we all know how lucky the Irish are—unless, of course, they're involved with the Southern Methodists!

INSTANT REPLAY

Jerry the Judge was right on the money in *Ake v. Oklahoma* and, as predicted, the Scarsdale Creche Committee fielded a nativity scene during the 1985 holiday season. Although Tennessee won the state playoff, it lost the Supreme Court battle in a case the judge called "a pick." But you can't win 'em all, and Jerry the Judge was caught off-side in the Albertini contest when the Supreme Court held for the Air Force base.

But two out of three keeps the judge in the winning column, and his best advice—keep your money in your wallet—keeps everyone even.

Nothing hits the spot after a good meal in a fine restaurant quite like having the parking attendant deliver your car with a spot that's been hit. Of course, having your coat given to the wrong person is almost as bad, and if your wife's new fur is stolen from the checkroom it's probably even worse than finding a dent in your car. Then, really to bring your blood to a boil, the owner often points to a sign in the lot or a statement on the claim check that says, "Management not responsible for damage or loss to checked items."

Well, the good news is that management is responsible and the law of bailments makes it so. When you leave that car or coat with the restaurant staff, you contract for care and attention. When they take your property they assume a duty to return it in the same shape as when it was delivered. That's what a bailment is all about.

The term *bailment* was borrowed by our English cousins from the French. It comes from the verb *bailler* and means to deliver. So, a bailment is the delivery of property to be held or used for a time and then returned to the owner. Your rental car, checked airline luggage, and the jewelry left in the hotel safe are all examples of bailments.

Like most things, bailments come in a variety of packages and with different responsibilities. The bailee is the person who holds your property and his duty of care depends upon who benefits. Where only you benefit, the holder must be careful but is liable only for gross negligence. Where both parties benefit, it's a mutual bailment and the holder must exercise ordinary care. But when only the holder benefits, he must exercise great care and is liable for even slight negligence. When you check your coat or car a mutual bailment is created.

Although the word *bailment* is relatively new, the principles involved in bailment law have been used for centuries and the basic provisions were outlined in the laws of Moses.

The ale houses and old inns of history always invited guests to enjoy food and lodging. Horses or camels or even dog sleds may have been parked or checked in days gone by and it was tough for an innkeeper to tell

Nanook that his wife's new bear coat had been given to the wrong Eskimo. Especially since Nanook didn't buy the coat, but took it from the bear! So if a coat was missing, or the carriage damaged, the innkeeper covered the cost. Yesterday it was a carriage, today it's a car. Different property, same rule.

So sign or no sign, statement or no statement, you're entitled to have your car delivered without any new dings or your coat returned after safekeeping. The claim check for your car or coat is only a token for identification. The disclaimer of responsibility is not part of your contract and is void.

Of course, if you park the car yourself or hang your coat on a hook outside the dining room, that's a different story. It's still a bailment, but the owner has less responsibility. But don't be intimidated by some claim check message or sign on the wall. If you think the negligence of the parking attendant or the innkeeper caused damage to your property, you can do something about it and you don't have to be as tough as Nanook. It's true that the law is sometimes a bear, but this bear can fight for you.

One of the most frightening promises of Orwell's *1984* was a society without privacy. Big Brother's giant computer holds your innermost secrets to be used whenever you become a threat or thorn. Fortunately, we don't have Big Brother watching us, but we do have an Uncle Sam that keeps pretty good track of us.

If you have ever been arrested, served in the military, or gone through a security check, you are a record in some federal agency. If you applied for a student loan, farm subsidy, medicare benefit, or worked for a federal agency, some Washington bureau has your name in its file. So in 1974 to keep Big Brother living only in the pages of Orwell's fiction, Congress passed the Privacy Act. That act gives you some control over what information the government gathers and how it's used and gives you a way to check the information being held in Washington's computer banks.

The Privacy Act allows you to review almost any federal file as long as it's a personal record on you kept by the executive branch. It also requires the government to keep the information confidential, and disclosure without your okay is a criminal offense. If you think there's a record on you in some federal agency, you can find out for sure. Just write, telephone, or go to the agency. If they have a file on you, they must say so and they must permit you to review that file.

If you make a written request, tell officials you want to review your file as authorized by the Privacy Act and write "Privacy Act Request" on the envelope. Since most agencies require proof of identification before they'll send record copies, be sure to sign the letter and include your social security number. And don't try to get information under false pretense about someone else or you'll end up in jail.

If the agency refuses your request, it must

explain why. You don't have to prove you need to know; the agency must prove its need to keep the record secret. If the agency says no, you can appeal, first with a letter to the agency and then in the federal courts.

The act requires that your agency record be complete, accurate, relevant and up-to-date. If you think its wrong, you can challenge the record and should ask the agency to correct it. Information about your religious or political activities or how you exercise First Amendment rights is none of the government's business and should not be part of your record. If the agency refuses to make changes, you must be told why and, again, you can appeal to the agency and then the courts.

You may have to pay the costs of copying your records, but not for time spent searching for or preparing the records. You can set a limit on the amount you're willing to pay and if costs are too high, you can ask the agency to reduce the costs. The records must also be given to you in a form that's "comprehensible," which means the bureau's gobbledegook must be eliminated or explained.

Of course, certain records are exempt from the act, such as CIA records or law enforcement files kept for criminal surveillance or prosecution. But parts of even CIA and FBI records can be released; and if the agency says no, it must show why the record should be withheld.

The Privacy Act of 1974 is an important weapon in the personal liberty arsenal. Few gov-

ernments have even permitted citizens such wide license in checking records of its executive agencies. So, use it, but don't abuse it! If you want more information, a "Citizens Guide" is available for a few dollars from the Government Printing Office in Washington, D.C. 20420.

When the Tons of Fun Club finishes a jazzercise session, some members run for the nearest coffee shop to refuel. But others make a beeline to the nearest doctor to help get their bodies through the rest of the day. Exercise may or may not be good for your health, but for the health care people the fitness fad has been terrific. The waiting rooms of M.D.'s, D.O.'s, chiropractors, podiatrists, and physical therapists are filled with folks from the exercise classes.

Today more people than ever before are involved in recreational exercise. Fitness centers, health spas, and aerobic dance groups are springing up everywhere. TV spots promote the more elaborate programs, while word of mouth spreads the time and dates of jazzercise sessions in school gyms or Jay-Cee halls.

Americans who feel the need to tone up and slim down assume their exercise centers are properly run by people who know what they're doing. Unfortunately, that's not always true. The only bottoms some owners are concerned with are the bottom lines of financial sheets. That often means poorly supervised programs, second-rate equipment, and unsafe facilities. After a few sessions, folks head for the local bone cracker with muscle and joint problems.

If you're in a fitness program, you have a legal right to expect it to be safe and operators have a legal duty to protect you and your body during exercise sessions. Instructors, for example, should at least be certified in CPR by the Red Cross or Heart Association. First aid equipment should be on hand along with a physician's emergency call list. Equipment should be inspected, properly maintained, and tested. Easy-to-read, step-by-step instructions should be posted for people using such items as rowing machines, exercise bikes, and nautilus power units. These "how to" procedures should alert users to machine risks and potential problems, and the staff should instruct and watch while you use any of the trendy new exercise units.

Program operators are also responsible for floor surfaces. Oily or overly waxed floors cause falls and skin burns, and aerobic sessions usually call for floor mats. You should be told the needed mat size and thickness; permitting you to exercise without a mat or with the wrong mat is negligence.

Serious diseases can be transmitted in unsanitary steam rooms, hot tubs, and saunas. Two people in a five hundred gallon hot tub is like two hundred in a 20 × 40 foot pool. Nationwide there were 1,100 spa-related emergency room injuries treated in 1980 and 30 spa-related deaths in 1981. Poorly covered suction drains, overexposure to heat, and use of hot tubs while under the influence of alcohol cause most injuries and that boils down to poor supervision.

The number of lawsuits grows each year as exercisers become more aware of their rights and discover exactly what exercise caused their injuries. So, check out instructor qualifications, equipment and facilities before you join an aerobic program or fitness center. Watch what releases you sign and remember that operators are responsible for negligence regardless of what any contract might say.

If you think your body needs toning up or slimming down, pick a program that will help, not hurt. And before you do any exercise, remember the words of Chauncey Depew, an American lawyer who at 94 said, "I get all the exercise I need by serving as pallbearer for my friends who exercise daily."

Buying a home may be the biggest investment you'll ever make and its sale may bring your largest capital gain. To make the most of this investment, you should be familiar with real estate procedures, financing methods, and the legal aspects of the purchase or sale.

Most people work with a real estate agency and sign a listing agreement. That's a legal contract which covers items like brokers' fees, the rights of the seller to negotiate the sale, and the terms restricting rights to sell. There are several types of listing agreements, but the one most often used gives one broker the exclusive right to sell for a specified time. The broker gets a commission if anyone sells the property within that time. Since that's a good deal for the broker, you have a right to expect his agency to advertise your property widely and to spend time and effort showing your property.

After a buyer is found you need a sales contract. It should spell out the purchase price, down payment, and the method of payment including financing plans. It should list what appliances, furnishings, fixtures, and other personal property will be sold with the house and should outline when utility bills and taxes shift between the parties and how taxes are to be prorated.

Real estate agents normally have a general sales contract. Review it with your attorney before signing or add the phrase, "Subject to approval by attorney within 'X' number of days." If you decide to use the agent's ready-made sales agreement, fill in all the blanks and make everything as specific as possible. For instance, if you're worried about the interest rate, spell out in the sales contract the maximum financing charge you will pay. Just saying "subject to adequate financing" may create rather than solve problems.

If you're selling you may want to limit warranties on the roof, the furnace, and certain appliances. If you're buying, you should ask whether warranties still exist on recent repairs or on new items and if these warranties can be transferred.

Buyers should insist on a marketable title. That means one free from indebtedness or

limitations on its use. It's up to the buyer to examine the title, and this should be done before the purchase is completed. A title search or examination of the records should be done and a certificate issued showing any problems with the title. You also need to check zoning laws and deed restrictions to see if they limit what you can do with the property. Maybe you want to open a day care center or convert into a two-family dwelling. Zoning or deed restrictions may say no.

Most of us borrow money to purchase a home and a lender will require title insurance in the amount of the loan. But that insurance doesn't protect you from any defects in the title. Owner's title insurance should be purchased to guarantee your equity in the property.

High interest rates of past years produced "creative financing" methods, including land contracts and renegotiable rate mortgages. Before you buy under any creative financing method, be sure you understand every aspect of these nonconventional loans. Don't sign without a review by your attorney.

Owning a home is part of the great American Dream. Don't let it become a nightmare. Considering the importance and the money involved, the best advice is to work with a lawyer from the beginning.

The old saying that life begins at forty may be true if your career is on the right track. But if you're forty or more and looking for work, you've got problems. Age discrimination, like sex and race bias, is part of the reality of life. The social problems created by age prejudice prompted Congress to make people aged forty to seventy a special class protected by the Age Discrimination and Employment Act.

That act protects you from arbitrary age discrimination at work. You cannot be threatened, forced to take a less responsible job, given fewer privileges, paid less, or treated differently from other, younger workers. No pension plan or seniority system can require you to retire involuntarily before the legal limit.

The law also encourages employment of people between ages forty and seventy. If you're qualified for a new job, it's illegal to discriminate in hiring on the basis of age unless age is a bonafide qualification. Playing the stage or TV role of a youngster, for example, requires an actor of a certain age and is a legitimate exception.

If you're changing careers in that forty to seventy age group, you must be given equal consideration with other qualified applicants regardless of age, and tax-supported employment agencies must refer you to any job for which you are qualified. Employers are forbidden to hold back promotions because of age, and policies of not promoting workers over a certain age have been declared illegal. Employers are also prohibited from discriminating against older workers in layoff or rehiring practices.

If you think you're a victim of age discrimination, you can file a "charge" with the Equal Opportunities Employment Commission. The complaint must be in writing with your name, age, and the name of the company you're charging. The EEOC will then try to mediate. If that fails, an investigation will begin and charges filed in federal court for violations of any federal law.

When Congress passed the Age Discrimination and Employment Act in 1975, it opened opportunities for education and training that once were denied. Universities receiving federal financial assistance cannot deny admission based on age, and both old and young are eligible for all student aid programs. Job and vocational training programs must also serve all age groups. Other federal legislation attempts to protect the financial security of older Americans with laws regulating credit, pension, insurance claims, and social security.

But let's not fool ourselves. These laws haven't ended age discrimination any more than the Civil Rights Act ended race discrimination. But they help and at least give older Americans a chance to be heard.

Former Ohio Senator Steve Young told his colleagues during the ADEA debate, "We don't grow old merely by living a number of years. We grow old by losing enthusiasm, deserting ideals, and abandoning the joy for life. Years may wrinkle the skin," he added, "but to abandon enthusiasm wrinkles the soul and deadens the brain."

So, if you're between forty and seventy, don't think the ball game is over. Congressman Claude Pepper at 83 is an active political campaigner. Pablo Picasso was painting at 91, and so was Grandma Moses at 101. Arturo Toscanini was still conducting at 87, Verdi wrote *Falstaff* at age 80, and Konrad Adenauer was Chancellor of West Germany at age 87. And speaking of political leaders, let's not forget that elderly chap in Washington named Ronald Reagan.

Buy now, pay later plans are as American as Mom's apple pie. "Charge-it" has become the national password, and Americans have played the credit game so well that consumer credit spending stands at over $1 trillion. But despite the ease with which most people get credit, some folks have trouble, particularly women and older Americans.

When you apply for credit, the creditor has the right to certain information, including your work history, job description, length of service, and salary. You may also have to provide information about such expenses as mortgage payments, utilities, and monthly credit obligations. Your credit history will be examined to determine if you pay bills regularly and how often you borrow money.

But some things are none of the creditor's business, and the Equal Credit Opportunity Act protects you from credit discrimination. It's a violation of that law to refuse or reduce credit based on age or sex. If you are an older American, you may not have your credit cancelled or be forced to reapply for credit simply because you have lived longer than some others. The same act protects women against discrimination based on sex and marital status. Women need not use Ms., Miss, or Mrs. on any credit application, and it's improper to ask about birth control practices or plans for children. A woman may not be required to have her husband cosign a credit application except in community property states, and if an application is based solely on her own income it is improper for a creditor to ask about the husband's income. It's also against regulations to require a woman to reapply for credit simply because her marital status changes.

When you apply for credit, you should be told within thirty days if the application has been approved or denied. If it is denied you're entitled to a written explanation of the reasons. If you think that you have been discriminated against, you should inform the creditor and if credit is still denied, you may wish to bring legal action.

It's your credit record and not age or sex that should determine whether your application is approved or denied. The Fair Credit Reporting Act allows you to check your credit with the agencies involved. If your application is denied, you may ask for the name and address of any agency that furnished credit information. You can then demand that the agency give you a copy of your file. If your credit report contains false, incomplete, or obsolete data, you can challenge its accuracy and the bureau must re-check. Any information more than seven years old should be deleted and a bankruptcy should be removed after ten years.

In 1983 my wife was denied a credit card. She is a career woman with an executive position and an independent income. She challenged the turn down and demanded the information which the company used. It looked like a case of sex discrimination. She contacted the company's national office and suggested that they reevaluate her application before she filed legal action. Within a week she had a credit card and a letter welcoming her as a new card holder. So, don't give up just because you get a no letter. If you think there's sex or age discrimination, the law can help—but only you can make it work.

If your neighbor decided to raise pigs in his backyard, it wouldn't be long before you'd have your fill of the little oinkers. The noise, sight, and possibly the smell would soon have you looking for help. Or maybe the kid next door decided to turn the garage into an auto repair shop and the engine noise and fumes are about to send you up the wall. What do you do? You can sue for money damages, but that's really not the answer. You don't want a percentage of the pig farm income or the repair shop business. You want both the oinkers and the engines shut off. So how do you get help? Is there some legal way to put an end to the nuisance next door? The answer, of course, is yes, but instead of going to a law court, you need help from a court of equity.

Equity courts developed in Old England alongside the common law courts. But the common law courts were very formal, would only handle certain cases, and awarded money damages. The equity courts, on the other hand, were less formal, were available to the poor, and developed remedies other than just awards of money. The equity courts were called the king's conscience and were nearly always headed by a clergyman.

Injunctions, specific performance, and declaratory judgments are examples of equity court remedies. For the nuisance next door, you don't want money from the law court—you want an injunction from the equity court. You want the court to tell the neighbor to close the auto shop or to get rid of the pigs. Then, if the neighbor fails to comply, it doesn't just cost him money, but he may go to jail for contempt of court.

Specific performance is another equity remedy. If, for some reason, the family heirloom falls into the wrong hands and you want it back, equity is the answer. Again, you don't want money, you want the heirloom, and the equity courts can force its return under penalty of jail.

A contract entered into by mutual mistake can be reformed by an equity court. Mandamus actions can force public officials to do certain things, and your legal rights can be outlined by an equity court in a declaratory judgment. Equity injunctions are often used in times of labor unrest to set the number of pickets and to prohibit the blockage of streets and entrances.

The concept of equity has played an important role in both the English and American legal systems. Today, however, the equity and common law courts have been combined. In most states, one judge presides over both courts and in the same courtroom. But even though the judge and court are combined, the powers and procedures are different. For example, when you sue in the equity court, you can't have a jury.

You are probably familiar with many of the one-liners from Parkinson's Law and Murphy's Law—such statements as, "If it ain't broke, don't fix it," or "If anything can break, it will break." Over the years, certain one-line statements of equity law—called maxims—have also been developed. They're not as funny as Murphy's Laws, but they're just as true. "He who comes to equity must come with clean hands," is an example, which leads to the saying, "Equality is equity."

If you have a problem that can't be solved with just plain old money, equity may offer an answer. But remember, equity courts are courts of conscience and be guided by the maxim "He who seeks equity must do equity."

When somebody drops an ipso facto between his res ipsa loquiturs, the odds are that somebody is a lawyer. We don't always understand what that person says and sometimes suspect he doesn't either, but we accept the lingo as part of the lawyer's professional mystique.

So it's really out of character to hear the pin-striped suit set talk about a strike force, a midnight raid, radar alerts, and preemptive strikes. That's Pentagon talk. And when they threaten to use pac man, the crown jewels, greenmail, and golden parachutes, it sounds like arcade game room talk. But it's really all part of the new corporate takeover jargon. Mergers and takeover struggles have made the business boardroom a battlefield. Over $100 billion changed hands in merger and takeover actions in the period from 1983 to 1985. And since business news has moved from the *Wall Street Journal* to the front pages of the local gazette, it might be fun to review the lawyers' new battle vocabulary.

Corporate lawyers now talk about black knights and white knights and crown jewels. The black knights are the folks trying to capture a corporation's assets. The crown jewels are the main assets of the company and could be a profitable division, a tax loss, or a new product. The people protecting the assets are white knights.

A corporate midnight raid begins when the Stock Exchange closes. Black knights try to line up stock pledges before the market reopens or the target company knows there's a raid. It's part of a blitz or lightening strike aimed at overwhelming the company. But corporations have a radar alert or early warning system to signal the coming of a takeover bid. Then the killer bees go into action. That's a group made up of the lawyer, banker, finance officer, public relations firm, and proxy solicitor. Their job is to fight a takeover, and companies tell black knights about killer bees to scare off corporate attacks. The offensive equivalent of the killer bees is the strike force.

Efforts to discourage hostile takeovers include the scorched earth plan in which a company sells off its more attractive assets. The crown jewels, for instance, are sold with a big cash dividend paid to stockholders.

Then there's not much left for the raiding company. The Jonestown defense is also used, but it's a suicidal tactic. Bankruptcy is an example of the Jonestown defense.

The hostile corporate takeover

With the pac man option, the white knights make an offer, equally hostile, to buy the stock of the attacking company. It's an "I'll eat you before you eat me defense." Sometimes black knights use greenmail. They buy a chunk of stock, threaten a takeover, and sell the shares back for a huge profit. But one of the neat tricks in the booby trap bag of the white knights is the golden parachute. That's a contract provision which gives huge severance pay to top executives in a takeover. One corporation gave its chief $8 million as a golden parachute. If a corporation protects all its executives, there won't be much operating capital left.

Takeover attempts have become as popular as their arcade game vocabulary, and the 2,500 corporate mergers of 1983 substituted battle language for the normal legalese. But while lawyers may sound like they're planning an attack, you don't have to circle the wagons yet! There is one area, however, where the legal eagles may have a problem. Some lawyers talk about their line of arbitrageurs. If that's anything like the line of Maginot, someone's going to be in deep serious trouble.

When Mortimer Caplan was director of the Internal Revenue Service, he said that the one difference between a tax collecter and a taxidermist was that the taxidermist would leave the hide. He probably thought that was funny, but most taxpayers think it's the truth and find very little to laugh about when it comes to paying taxes or working with the IRS.

Sure some taxpayers receive refunds each year, but thousands of others receive a Statutory Notice of Deficiency. That's about as welcome as a draft notice. It tells a taxpayer that more money is due and to pay up or else. The "or else" creates visions of iron bars and prison walls, so most folks just go ahead and pay up. But there's really a lot more to the "or else" than a jail cell, and the options are worth checking out. First of all, the "or else" includes a complete appeal procedure within the IRS itself that's really pretty good. If you don't like the idea of appealing to the people who already decided you owe more money, there's a neat way for you to get your case into a court, and it's an informal and inexpensive way to boot!

In 1968, the U.S. Tax Court created something called the Small Case Division. It's a lot like the People's Court of Judge Wapner's that you see on TV. A $60 filing fee will put you on the court's small case docket and since the government is used to dealing in big bucks, a small case to the tax court is anything less than $10,000.

If you decide you want to use the court's small case program, you can get a set of fill-in-the-blank petition forms by writing to the U.S. Tax Court in Washington, D.C. Preparing the court petition is a lot easier than filling out your annual tax return.

When you have your hearing, you can represent yourself at the trial and the procedures will be informal. No opening or closing arguments are necessary and you won't be asked to write any complicated legal briefs. Since tax court judges travel the country and hold their hearings in federal courtrooms, you can even choose the city where your case will be heard.

But just because the trial procedures are informal doesn't mean that there are no procedures at all. You still have to do something to show that you're right and the bureau's wrong. So, if you have receipts or papers or documents that support your claim, bring them to the hearing. Remember that information you may have sent to the IRS is not part of the court file.

You can't file your small tax case until you've received the official Statutory Notice of Deficiency from the IRS, and when you do get that notice, you have only ninety days to file your petition. If you should lose the case in tax court, you can't appeal; but if the IRS loses, it can't appeal either.

Because the tax court usually has about a ten thousand case backlog, it may be six months to a year before you actually get to court. But the only cost of that delay is the interest on any tax you may have to pay. So all things considered, the tax court's small case program is a pretty decent "or else" option. It still won't make the IRS or paying taxes funny, but tax court judges are not tax collectors, so they won't take your hide.

Oliver Wendell Holmes once told us, "Taxes are the price we pay for a civilized society," but Chief Justice Marshall reminded society that the power to tax was the power to destroy. Sometimes when the price of civiliza-

tion gets too high, society throws some rather uncivilized tea parties.

Thanks to the federal government, there's no longer any need for an awkward pause before you introduce the unmarried couple next door to family or friends. When they arrive at your next cocktail party, you can just say, "This is my neighbor Jane and her Posslq, Mike." Posslq, P-O-S-S-L-Q, is the census taker's acronym for a modern American lifestyle. The letters stand for "person other than spouse sharing living quarters."

Census figures show that from 1970 to 1979, the number of unmarried live-ins jumped from 520,000 to 1,346,000. Most are young people who have rejected the traditional marriage relationship. But figures also show a significant number of elderly Americans living as unmarried couples because marriage would decrease Social Security benefits and the live together arrangement is financially attractive.

For many years it was a crime for a single man and woman to live together and, in fact, it's still illegal in a few states. In Wisconsin it was considered deviant behavior and punishable with a $10,000 fine and up to nine months in prison. But even in the states that still consider living together a crime, the law is rarely enforced and when it is, fines are usually minor. Of course, at one time couples who lived together as man and wife became man and wife through something called a common law marriage. But most states today reject the common law rule and unmarried couples living together have few, if any, legal rights or obligations.

People often live together without marriage because they think it's easier to split up if things turn sour. It's true the unmarried couple can separate at will, but the fight begins when he or she leaves with the TV, VCR, or the bank book. Judges traditionally have refused to recognize agreements between unmarried live-ins. It was a crime and the relationship was illicit. If there was a contract, it was assumed to be based on sex and thrown out because it was against public policy.

After all, the family unit was basic to American society and marriage was the foundation of the family. So the legal system went out of its way to discourage the live-in arrangement. But then the California courts and movie star Lee Marvin gave America its first "palimony" award. The court recognized the right of unmarried live-ins to have enforceable contracts regarding the ownership and division of property.

Unmarried couples still have no legal rights unless they create them, and the best way to do that is with a written contract. Some courts have applied partnership law to help protect parties without formal agreements, but without a written contract, it's a tough row to hoe for the party trying to share—and that's usually the woman.

Skyrocketing divorce rates and the increase in the number of posslqs have created much public concern about the future of the traditional marriage. But two-thirds of all U.S. adults are married and living with their spouse. So marriage as a social and legal institution is still alive and well in America.

But for those couples who choose the modern route, BEWARE! The old rule of the marketplace was caveat emptor, but in the kissing booths, the rule is caveat amator, which means "let the lover beware." If your sweetheart suggests sharing lives together, find out if that means sharing property, too. Then, put it in writing. It's not very romantic, but just as a paper towel seldom survives a trip to the laundry, love and romance seldom survive a trip to the courts.

A few years ago the motto in the work place was, "He whose bread I eat, his song I sing." In those days a whistle-blower was someone who signaled a lunch break or the end of the work day. To "fire at will" was a management way of life, not a military command, and companies operated on the philosophy that a worker produced in direct proportion to his fear of being fired.

But all that was before workers organized or got a conscience. Times change and in the work place of today it's not so easy to pass out the infamous pink slip. Now workers have legal rights to protect them from unjust discharges, and the boss often needs something called "just cause" before an employee can be fired.

During the industrial revolution, a common law rule developed which said an employer could hire at will and fire at will. That rule came to the new world with the Pilgrims and became the American way. The boss could fire an employee for "good cause" or "no cause." If a worker was told to do something he or she didn't like or that was illegal, the choice was to do it or quit.

But in 1935, the law began to change. First the Wagner Act made it illegal to fire a worker for joining or helping to organize a union. When the unions got established, they negotiated contracts which substituted "just cause" for "at will" to protect their members from unjust discharge. Other federal and state laws were adopted later to protect workers from being fired because of race, age, sex, religious belief, or physical handicap.

Even after the efforts of unions, the Congress, and various state assemblies, however, the old common law "hire and fire at will" rule still applied to nearly ninety million Americans. Perhaps it will always be with us and we need to recognize that the boss has rights, too.

Still, asking for "just cause" before the discharge of an employee isn't an unreasonable request, particularly in light of the consequences to the family and the community, so the courts got back into the act. Just as the courts of old developed the "at will" rule, the courts of today developed and modified the "just cause" rule. It's a rule based on a public policy or implied contract theory which protects workers not covered by a union contract or statute. An employee who can prove

his discharge violated a clear public policy can sue to recover the job along with back pay. These are today's whistle-blowers. Someone fired because of a refusal to falsify a food package label or one who wouldn't dump toxic waste in a local river is a whistle-blower. But it must be a clear public policy and, since the whistle-blower has the burden of proof, it's a tough case to win.

The implied contract is an easier route for a fired worker to follow. Even here the company must have done something to create the belief that a worker would not have been fired without just cause. Company policy statements, advertisements, job handbooks, inducements to leave an old job, and benefit plans can all be used by the fired worker to show that an implied contract existed.

So if you find yourself with a pink slip you can't wear or give to your spouse, don't despair. Some estimates say as many as 50 percent of all workers fired are fired for no good reason. If you ever think you're part of that 50 percent, you may be protected by a state or federal statute or you may have a public policy or implied contract lawsuit. Of course, you'll need an attorney, but some laws make the company pay your legal fees if you win. If you have a job problem, check with an attorney. It's kind of like chicken soup—it can't hurt!

If someone got "bumped off" in an old Jimmy Cagney or Humphrey Bogart movie, it meant he was killed. The evil-eyed gangsters in those grade B flicks were forever planting people in the East River or using their trusty "gat" to bump off a good guy cop or a crusading district attorney.

Fortunately, in real life it's not so easy to get bumped off, unless, of course, you're talking about air travel. Hundreds—maybe thousands—of good guy travelers get bumped off by airlines each year. They don't get eliminated; they just get delayed, frustrated, and suffer extra expenses.

The airlines bump you off when they oversell or overbook a flight. Then you and your ticket end up standing at the gate while the plane roars off into the wild blue yonder carrying only your baggage and your dreams. Not a good way to start a vacation and even worse if you're headed for a business meeting or a convention speech. So if there's some air travel in your future, it's time to learn your DBC's. DBC stands for delayed boarding compensation; that's the money the airline is required by law to pay if you're involuntarily denied boarding. You're entitled to twice the value of your flight to the next stopover or, if there are none, to the final destination up to a maximum of $400 as delayed boarding compensation. If the airline can arrange a flight that gets you to your destination or stopover within two hours after your original flight, you're still entitled to DBC, but the maximum is $200.

When there's an overbooking problem, the airline must provide a statement outlining your right to DBC, and before the airline can bump anyone, it must first ask for volunteers. If there are not enough volunteers, bumping may occur, but only according to a prearranged boarding plan, which you have a right to see. Airlines usually offer free air travel coupons to volunteers, but if you don't volunteer and get bumped, you're entitled to cash—on the spot! The airlines also usually pay such incidental expenses as long distance phone calls or the purchase of toilet articles.

Of course, you have some responsibilities before you're entitled to DBC. You must comply with all the airline rules regarding ticketing, reconfirmation, and check-in times. If not, you lose! Then, too, if the airline was forced to use a smaller plane because of a mechanical problem, it's off the hook. Also, if your ticket section is overbooked and you refuse to change sections, you can forget any DBC. But if your ticket is downgraded, you are entitled to a refund of the price difference.

When Allegheny Airlines unceremoniously bumped Ralph Nader from his flight, he was offered $32 in compensation, but he refused the money and elected to sue. The diplomatic genius of Allegheny cost the airline $25,000 when Nader won that lawsuit. You have the same right to sue, but if that's your plan, don't take the check or cash. If you accept the airline's payment, you may lose other legal remedies.

In fairness, air carriers do a pretty good job overall and they have their own set of problems. But if you've done everything you're supposed to do and still get bumped off, those airline people will look like Public Enemy #1. In that case be armed with your

DBC travel rights kit and don't be bashful at the ticket counter. Remember that great old legal maxim, "The squeaky wheel gets the grease!"

Americans have so loved the "buy now, pay later" plans that credit spending in the United States has reached the $1 trillion mark. But these easy credit policies produce unwanted side effects, and in 1981, 500,000 people filed personal bankruptcy—five times more than in the mid 1970s.

Monthly payments may seem small, but they still have an effect on the budget. So, once you decide to use credit, shop around for the best deal. Here are some terms that may be helpful.

Finance charges are the total dollars paid to use credit. It includes interest and such hidden costs as service charges or credit related insurance. The Annual Percentage Rate or APR is the annual rate of interest charged. The APR may be identical from creditor to creditor, but the method used to compute interest can make a difference in the finance charge. Shop for credit like any other item. Don't be afraid to ask how the financing charge is computed and what the total charge will be.

To decide if you're a good risk, creditors will examine your credit record. To establish that record start with a bank checking or savings account and a charge with a local store. As you move up the credit ladder, make pay-ments regularly and be certain your statements are correct. A billing mistake can hurt your rating. Maybe you were charged for something you didn't buy or items that you returned are still on your account. Other errors might include arithmetic mistakes or failure to record all your payments.

If you find an error, take immediate action. The Fair Credit Billing Act outlines ways to correct mistakes. Notify your creditor in writing of any error within sixty days. The creditor has thirty days to acknowledge your letter and two billing periods to correct the error or notify you why not.

If no error is found, you're entitled to a new statement of your account which can include finance charges. But if an error is found, finance charges can't be added on the disputed amount. Neither the creditor nor any credit bureau can give any credit information that would hurt your record while a dispute exists. But after the bill is corrected the creditor can take action to collect the account.

If you get behind in payments, you may hear from a collection agency. But the Fair Debt Collection Practices Act prohibits abusive, deceptive, or unfair practices by private collection firms. The agency may contact you by mail, in person, or by telephone during the day. But, if you notify the agency by mail not to contact you again, they must stop—except to tell you that legal action is under way.

The law also outlines the rules a collection agency must follow. Within five days of the first contact, the agency must tell you in writing the amount you owe, the creditor's name, and what you can do if you think there is an error. It's illegal to use false statements when attempting to collect a debt.

If you absolutely can't meet your debts, bankruptcy may be the final resort. But first review everything with an attorney. Different sections of the Bankruptcy Act offer several debt reduction plans. Before filing bankruptcy, go through a good credit counseling session and explore all the other avenues of debt relief.

According to the rules posted in an 1872 schoolhouse, teachers of the time were required to fill the lamps and clean the chimneys and bring a bucket of water and a scuttle of coal for each day's class session. Women teachers were reminded that if they married or engaged in unseemly conduct, they would be dismissed, while men, on the other hand, were encouraged to spend one or two nights a week courting the ladies.

Life in the twentieth-century classroom is a little better. The EPA won't let the schools burn coal, water is on tap, and lamps are lit with a flick of a switch. But classroom teachers are still plagued with their share of school board rules and state regulations. Most states now have specific statutes making it the legal duty of teachers to maintain good order and discipline in the school. Recent Gallup polls show the public thinks discipline is the number one problem of U.S. education; filling the lamps and cleaning the chimneys was prob-

ably an easier job than solving today's discipline problem.

Of course, in this litigious society, it was just a matter of time before mom, dad, the kids, and teachers found themselves in the courts. Disciplinary injuries to children cases lead the parade from today's schoolrooms to the courtrooms.

Because the law requires that teachers maintain order and discipline, it also gives them the authority to do the job. They have the legal right to make reasonable rules and regulations covering student behavior as well as the right to enforce those rules. The questions asked in court concern what is reasonable and how much actual physical force can be used.

Teachers, of course, have been using corporal or physical punishment to help keep order in the classroom at least since colonial times and probably longer. The Supreme Court has warned schools not to become little camps of fascism, but when the right to discipline a student physically has been questioned, the law generally sides with the teacher.

The use of a paddle across the fanny is not cruel and unusual punishment and doesn't violate due process. So if little Johnny or Suzie comes running home with a red bottom, don't rush to see your lawyer unless the force used was so unreasonable that it caused some serious injury. The law doesn't ask our teachers to give notice or hold a hearing before spanking an unruly child. It asks only that they be fair and reasonable. Before using the paddle, teachers should consider the nature of what the student has done wrong, as well as the student's age, sex, past behavior, and mental and physical health. They should also be careful with what they use to carry out the punishment. A wooden paddle is one thing, a whip is another. And a teacher who paddles in anger or out of malice is probably asking for an injury lawsuit.

Unfortunately, in some American classrooms there's a better chance of teacher abuse than student abuse. The law tries to support the teachers, but a little help from parents would probably be welcomed. The great English writer Samuel Johnson once said, "There is now less flogging in our great schools, but then less is learned there; so what the boys get at one end, they lose at the other." And so it would seem that great legal maxim, "Spare the rod and spoil the child," applies equally well in the schoolroom as in the living room.

In 1933, the constable of a small western town pinched the Fuller Brush man for soliciting without a license. A few years later when the Supreme Court of that state upheld the salesman's conviction, the little town of Green River, Wyoming became famous. Communities throughout the nation adopted their own version of the Green River Ordinance in an early attempt to protect the American consumer. In the years to follow, the Fuller Brush man would become a welcome visitor to most American households and, by comparison, he was a prince among door-to-door salesmen.

Although most doorbell peddlers were decent, honest folks, some combined fast talk and high pressure tactics to force people to buy. By the time some people got their doors closed, they were saddled with a host of unwanted books, appliances, soaps, and cosmetics. Finally, the Federal Trade Commission stepped in and gave the consumer something called a cooling-off period. Most states followed the FTC example, which gives the consumer three days to cancel any door-to-door contract if second thoughts arise about the purchase. The law also requires doorbell peddlers to advise people of their three-day right to cancel, and if they don't, the sale is voidable.

That's just one example of the legal protections available to the modern consumer. False advertising, phony contests, fake prizes, free gift gimmicks, and the old bait and switch schemes are all illegal and consumer laws offer protection. Of course, not all advertising is false or all contests phony. For example, an ad offering to sell you the "World's Greatest Used Car" is not false, but just something called salesman's puffing. It may not be the world's greatest car, but the seller is entitled to his opinion and it's not likely that ad would deceive you. On the other hand, an advertisement for a genuine leather wallet that turns out to be made of plastic is false and illegal.

The phone call or letter that says you have just won a free mattress and all you have to do is buy the bed probably also violates federal and state law. By the time you realize you've been had in some of these phony prize frauds, you have both the bed and a debt. The good news is that a contract you sign because of some fake prize gimmick can be cancelled.

One of the most frustrating consumer scams is the old bait and switch scheme. A super low priced color TV is advertised, but when you try to buy one the clerk says they just ran out or that the cheap model is lousy and you'd better buy a substitute, higher priced model. By the time the color fades on the peacock's feathers, you're out the door with a TV you didn't want and payments you can't afford. Again, thanks to consumer laws, you can put that bait and switch contract in the trash can and take the TV back to the store.

American consumers have flexed some big economic and political muscles. Some states have even created an Independent Consumer Protection Agency to investigate and handle public complaints. If you have a question or problem and need help, check with your county prosecutor, district attorney, or the state attorney general's office. Help is available. But after you've paid or signed a contract, the burden is on you to show deception or unfair practice. So, the old adage that an ounce of prevention is worth a pound of cure is still a good rule to remember and follow.